AN ANNOTATED DICTIONARY
OF TECHNICAL, HISTORICAL, AND STYLISTIC
TERMS RELATING TO THEATRE AND DRAMA

A Handbook of Dramaturgy

AN ANNOTATED DICTIONARY
OF TECHNICAL, HISTORICAL, AND STYLISTIC
TERMS RELATING TO THEATRE AND DRAMA

A Handbook of Dramaturgy

R. Kerry White

The Edwin Mellen Press
Lewiston/Queenston/Lampeter

Library of Congress Cataloging-in-Publication Data

White, R. Kerry.
   An annotated dictionary of technical, historical, and stylistic
terms relating to theatre and drama : a handbook of dramaturgy / R.
Kerry White.
      p.   cm.
   Includes bibliographical references and index.
   ISBN 0-7734-8989-4 (soft cover)
   ISBN 0-7734-8873-1 (hard cover)
   1. Theater--Dictionaries. 2. Drama--Dictionaries. I. Title.
PN2035.W48 1995
792'.03--dc20   95-7
                                                              CIP

A CIP catalog record for this book is available from the British Library.

Copyright © 1995 R. Kerry White

The Edwin Mellen Press   The Edwin Mellen Press
        Box 450   Box 67
   Lewiston, New York   Queenston, Ontario
   USA 14092-0450   CANADA L0S 1L0

                 The Edwin Mellen Press, Ltd.
                   Lampeter, Dyfed, Wales
                 UNITED KINGDOM SA48 7DY

           Printed in the United States of America

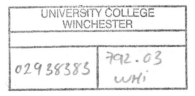

Dedication

To my wife, Margaret, for 25 years of theatre.

CONTENTS

ILLUSTRATIONS

PREFACE

Offstage Life, a Dramaturgical Dictionary is intended to supplement general encyclopedias such as the *Cambridge Guide to American Theatre* (Wilmeth and Miller, 1993) and historical surveys like Brockett's *History of the Theatre* (1991). Its specific purpose is to serve as a resource text and as an encouragement for a clarity of discourse about the conventions of drama, theatre and performance. In this regard, the *Dictionary* will be particularly useful to students of theatre history, dramatic theory and theatre aesthetics.

Unlike encyclopedias, the *Dictionary* does not include entries on specific people, plays or theatres, although many of each are cited as examples; unlike a history, the *Dictionary* does not follow a chronological sequence nor cite historical details of people, plays, productions or theatres for their own sakes, but much historical material is included. Unlike texts on dramatic theory, the *Dictionary* is not intended to provide detailed discussions of individual works or theorists, but of ideas and conventions.

The nearly 400 entries discuss the origins, meaning, historical significance and dramaturgical implications of several classes of theatrical terms. These include commonly (mis)used words such as "drama," "play," "theatre" and "performance;" technical terms such as "offstage life," "plot," "aside," and "deixis;" words commonly denoting theatrical style such as "realism," "expressionism" and "modernism;" and words specific to the various branches of dramaturgy.

Entries are cross referenced in **bold face** to facilitate the study of a line of related dramaturgical concepts and many refer the reader to illustrative diagrams which bring several connected terms together. For example, the word **theatre** is discussed in its several senses (event, tradition, building) and this leads one to **drama** and **performance** and these in turn lead to several other terms and illustrations. While some entries briefly define terms, many are short essays on the significance of complex ideas and theories, with references to specific plays and suggestions for further reading.

Of the many plays cited as examples, a few reappear in a variety of contexts: Sophocles' *Oedipus*, the Wakefield *Second Shepherd's Play*, Shakespeare's *King Lear*, Robertson's *Caste*, Ibsen's *Hedda Gabler*, Chekhov's *Cherry Orchard*, Hammerstein's *Oklahoma!*, and Beckett's *Waiting for Godot*. These are plays which any student of the theatre should know. An equal familiarity with the *Dictionary* will lead to an appreciation of the dramaturgy of the styles these plays exemplify.

Above all, the entries in this text are intended to provoke thought and discussion. For this reason many comments are deliberately provocative or at least raise issues and implications not normally considered.

I would like to acknowledge teachers who have provoked me with fresh insight and novel perspectives: Klauss Strassman (University of British Columbia), Alan Gowans (University of Victoria), Grant McKernie and Robert Trotter (University of Oregon). I would also like to acknowledge the pioneering effort done in this area by the late David E. Jones and his assistant, Jack Halstead of the University of Utah. Their "Dictionary of Dramaturgical Terms" (1988, unpublished) was a valuable guide for this dictionary.

A

AB OVO

(Latin: "from the egg," in Horace, *Ars Poetica*.[1] See also, ***in media res***: Latin, "in the middle of things.") These two phrases refer to structural strategies: to begin the **action** of a play at the beginning of the **fable** (story) and to proceed to the end; or to begin in the middle of the events of the fable and to proceed with a combination of **exposition** and current action. The former is illustrated in medieval **mystery cycles**, the latter in plays with classical structures (the prototype being Sophocles' *Oedipus*).

ABSURDISM

"Absurdism" refers to a subcategory of **modernism**, with specific application to certain post WW II playwrights, such as Arthur Adomov, Samuel Beckett, Alfred Camus, Eugene Ionesco and others. The term was coined by Martin Esslin to describe the plays produced by these playwrights which tend to reflect the influence of contemporary existential philosophy as well as a post war nihilism.[2]

Absurdist theatre in general (if such an abstraction is possible) represents a strong denial of the relevance of western philosophy, religion and aesthetics. To the absurdists, logic and even the languages used to express "logical thought" are not

---

[1]Horace, "The Art of Poetry," 147-149, trans. by Edward Henry Blakeney, in Bernard Dukore, ed., *Dramatic Theory and Criticism* (New York: Holt, Rinehart and Winston, 1974), p. 71.

[2]Martin Esslin, *Theatre of the Absurd* (New York: Grove, 1960).

only suspect, they are contaminated by the artificiality and rigidity of their own assumptions and rules. Human behaviour in an "absurd" universe may be influenced by heredity and environmental factors (see **naturalism**), but action is seen to be meaningless. Art, and especially dramatic and theatrical art, therefore tends to present itself self-consciously as a metaphor of human existence in a world without absolutes. (See also **metatheatre**.) At best, life is a constant struggle in vain between subjective personalities for communication. In his critical essay, *Proust*, Samuel Beckett sounded the death knell of traditional character communication:

> Even on the rare occasions when word and gesture happen to be valid expressions of personality, they lose their significance in their passage through the cataract of the personality that is opposed to them. Either we speak and act for ourselves--in which case speech and action are distorted and emptied of their meaning by (the other) or else we speak and act for others--in which case we speak and act a lie.[3]

With the absurdists, **drama**, as "human relationships in crisis," took on new meaning.

(See also Enoch Brater and Ruby Cohn, eds., *Around the Absurd: Essays on Modern and Post Modern Drama*, 1990.)

ACTION

This is a particularly slippery concept made worse by the ambiguities of the English language. In dramaturgy, *action,* as a singular noun, comes from Aristotle's definition of tragedy: "a tragedy . . . is an imitation of an action . . . ."[4] It is an attempt to locate the unifying **objective** of a play as a whole: a *gestalt*. A play's *action* is not so much independent of **character** objectives as the synergistic result of their combination. *Action* is to drama what central theme is to narrative. Thus, the action of *Oedipus* might be expressed in an infinitive phrase: "to find the killer

---

[3]Samuel Beckett, *Proust (*New York: Grove, 1957), p. 46.

[4]Aristotle, *Poetics,* translated by Ingram Bywater (New York: Random House, 1947), chap. 6, 1449a, 25-28. Note: further references to the *Poetics* will be by chapter, manuscript page and line number.

of Laius," or "to reveal the identity of Oedipus," which we learn is the same thing in the end.[5]

Unity of action is achieved through the *internal relevance* of all characters, **issues** and incidents. To Aristotle, an action was "complete" if it had a beginning, a middle and an end and if each of the incidents in its **plot** was causally related to the others. It is in this sense that the *end* of a play's action is contained in its *beginning*.

ACTING, ACTOR

These terms imply a element of **impersonation**, which makes an actor and acting a sub-category of **performance**. The history of the theatre (i.e., **performance dramaturgy**) is the history of actors and acting: techniques, conditions, social status, exemplary artists and performances, and gender bias.

The terms also imply an **audience**, the second element in the **performance triad** (the third being some form of text). Indeed, purists such as Jerzy Grotowski have insisted on the unencumbered presence of the actor facing an audience as the essence of **theatre**.[6]

AESTHETIC DISTANCE

This is a concept which attempts to characterize the gaze of the spectator when viewing a work of art. The work itself has internal **conventions** which set it apart from everyday reality, thus giving the observer a "detached" perspective on the observed. The convention of the proscenium arch, for example, *distances* a play from surrounding space/time reality. Paradoxically, the conventions of a **representational style**, such as **realism**, which attempts to create an illusion of empirical reality, are *distanced* and thus countered by the stage frame. On the other hand, a **presentational style** pretends to break through this frame to address the audience

---

[5]Francis Fergusson, *The Idea of a Theatre* (New York: Doubleday, 1949), pp. 243-44.

[6]Jerzy Grotowski, *Towards a Poor Theatre* (New York: Simon and Schuster, 1968), p. 15

directly, thus threatening to destroy the *aesthetic distance*. Other conventions (of acting style, of costume, of time and space, etc.), however, simultaneously work to maintain *distance*, thus creating a dramaturgical tension between "actuality" and "art." The conventions of **modernist art** and **metatheatre** play with this tension, on the one hand by foregrounding the characteristics of the medium, while on the other by including representational elements. (See also *verfremdungseffect.*)

Some modern theorists who have considered the principle of *aesthetic distance* from various disciplinary points of view include: Edward Bullough ("Psychical Distance as a Factor in Art and Aesthetic Principle," in *British Journal of Psychology*, V, 1912); Susan K. Langer (*Feeling and Form*, 1953); Erving Goffman (*Frame Analysis*, 1961) and Daphna Ben Chaim (*Distance in the Theatre*, 1984).

AESTHETICISM

See **modernism** and **art for art's sake.**

AGON

(Greek: "contest".) Originally *agon* referred to state sponsored musical contests. In drama, formally, *agon* refers to the "contest" between opposing characters in their roles as **agents** of the **action** (see **protagonist** and **antagonist**). Often, in Greek theatre, each side is supported by half of the chorus.

More profoundly, *agon* refers to a fundamental dramaturgical principle, namely, that an individual's notions of reality and truth (which condition his personal **objectives**) produce conflicts with the ideas/beliefs/objectives of others. **Drama**, in this sense, imitates the essence of the human condition. (See also **absurdism**.)

ALAZON

(Greek: "imposter.") The *Alazon* is the "braggart" role in ancient comedy (also *miles gloriosus*, or "braggart warrior"); he is cited as one of the three archetypes of comic character in the anonymous Roman MS, *Tractatus Coislinianus* (see also, *eiron, bromolochus*).[7]

In terms of **social function**, the objective of comedy is the correction of unacceptable behaviour, often through ridicule. Therefore, to brag is to represent yourself falsely and this makes you an imposter and a subject of public censure.

ALIENATION-EFFECT

See *verfremdungseffect* and **epic theatre**; see also figure 6.

ALTERNATIVE THEATRE

Theatre opposed to "mainstream" or "establishment" theatre *in form as well as content*, "marginalized" or "fringe" theatre. "Opposed to" is perhaps an important distinction: there have always been forms of theatre existing outside of the mainstream. Comedy, for example, was not officially recognised in Athenian dramatic festivals until around 487 BC, and comedy not only satirized the icons of the Athenian establishment, it also exhibited a radical structure.

However, since establishment theatres and plays received official support, both legal and financial, they and their dramaturgical traditions have been preserved through documentation, while alternative theatres and plays have all too often disappeared from the historical record. On the other hand, evidence of the parallel existence of alternative styles and forms is frequently evident in their influences on mainstream theatre.

The modern alternative theatre "movement" began in the 1890's with such small independent theatre companies as Antoine's Theatre Libre in Paris, Grein's Independent Theatre in London and Brahm's Die Freie Buhne in Berlin. These were formed to produce the unconventional and often censored works of playwrights like

---

[7]Anonymous, *Tractatus Coislinianus*, translated by Lane Cooper, in Dukore, *Dramatic Theory and Criticism*, pp. 64-66.

Strindberg and Ibsen.

More recently, the alternative theatre in England began with protest plays such as the "fringe" productions at the Edinburgh Festival in the early 1970's. The "Off Broadway" theatres in post WW II New York and especially the "Off Off Broadway" movement of the 1960's were protests against the high costs of commercial theatre. The works presented in these non-traditional spaces catered to counter-culture audiences. Individual companies with wider national and international bases, such as the San Francisco Mime Troupe, The Living Theatre and the Bread and Puppet Theatre began as marginal enterprises, but through success--especially among the "radical chic" and university audiences--became part of an avant-garde establishment.

(See T. Shank, *American Alternative Theatre*, 1982; Peter Ansorge, *Disrupting the Spectacle: Five years of Experimental and Fringe Theatre in Britain,* 1975; Margaret Croyden, *Lunatics, Lovers and Poets: the Contemporary Experimental Theatre,* 1974.)

In Canada, the alternative theatre movement began in the 1960's, as much a product of a growing class of university trained theatre artists as anything else (although OFY and LIPP grants from the Canada Council and Canada's centennial played their part as well). The movement was responsible for numerous companies across the country whose productions broke with traditional dramaturgy (see **collective creations** and **popular theatre**). Many of these plays were not only original, they also had a distinctly Canadian focus. The culmination of the movement in Canada, ironically, has been the phenomenally successful "fringe festivals," which began in Edmonton in 1981--ironic because success has turned these festivals (now a virtual summer network) into tourist attractions for the establishment.

(See Renate Usmiani, *Second Stage: the Alternative Theatre Movement in Canada,* 1968; Alan Filewod, *Collective Encounters: Documentary Theatre in English Canada,* 1987.)

AMBIGUITY

A basic principle of aesthetics, ambiguity refers to the potential interpretations of an artistic **code**. The three basic channels of the theatrical **multi-modal communication system** (aural, visual and kinetic sign systems) not only have built-in redundancy, they are individually open to a variety of interpretations. It is the connotative power, or *ambiguity* of signs that facilitates the joint creativity of artist and spectator. In the theatre, the variety of audience response to such signs compounds the ambiguity of the message: each member brings a different decoding potential to the work (see **reception theory**). Limits to ambiguity, on the other hand, are created by the syntactical relationships among signs and among sign (or code) systems: that is, one sign can limit or qualify the ambiguity of another.

As a co-ordinating interpreter of this system, the stage director attempts to control the potential ambiguity of the performance and to guide the audience's attention in order to limit what might otherwise be an incoherent jumble of cross modal signs. Similarly, the other artists involved in a production attempt to define the parameters of the ambiguity of their work. The designer through shape, colour, texture, line, light and shade, limits the potential interpretations of the text to specific historical, cultural and aesthetic areas; the actor, in developing a unique character (not Hamlet, but Olivier's Hamlet), attempts to make the general as specific as possible with every line, gesture and movement.

The first major attempt to deal with this subject (in English) was in the area of literary criticism.

(See William Empson, *Seven Types of Ambiguity*, 1930); other useful discussions are included in Susan K. Langer, *Philosophy in a New Key*, 1951; Umberto Eco, *A Theory of Semiotics*, 1976; Kier Elam, *The Semiotics of Theatre and Drama*, 1980.)

ANAGNORISIS

(Greek: "recognition.") A fundamental convention of Aristotelian dramaturgy (and classical drama) referring to the point in a tragedy's **plot** when the true identity of the hero is made known and/or when the significance of events is manifest (for example, when the identity of Oedipus is recognized by everyone involved, along with an awareness of the consequences of past actions). It is at this point that the hero is also recognized as a *tragic* hero. According to Aristotle (*Poetics*), this moment logically should coincide with the *peripeteia* (turning point) of the **action**.[8]

ANTAGONIST

(Greek: "opposing contestant.") The character who opposes the **protagonist's** ("hero's") objective and/or the **action** of the play. In a strict sense, **drama** requires an antagonist for its existence, although such a character may not be physically present, as in single character plays. (See also **deuteragonist.**)

ANTI-CLIMAX

See **climax**.

ANTI-MASQUE

Created by Ben Jonson at the suggestion of Queen Henrietta (*The Masque of Queens*, 1609), the anti-masque injected the dramaturgical element of contest (see *agon*) into the strictly celebratory form of the **masque**. The anti-masque is generically related to the **satyr play**, which in turn is the archetype of **farce**.

In Jonson's masques, the anti-masquers were grotesque creatures played by *professionals* (the masquers themselves were courtiers). These barbarians, who disrupted the smooth progress of the masque's **plot**, opposed the hero and were seen as threats to the perfect state being established on stage (and thus as symbolic threats to the "perfect" court being celebrated in the audience). Banishing these imperfect creatures from the stage (and the common actors from the hall) restored peace and harmony to both spaces. This then prepared the way for the celebratory conclusion

---

[8]Aristotle, *Poetics*, chap. 13, 1452b, 33.

of the masque, a dance (see **revels**) between courtly performers and their ladies in the audience.

(See Stephen Orgel, *The Masques of Ben Jonson*, 1978 and *The Illusion of Power*, 1975.)

ANTI-STROPHE

See **Strophe.**

APRON STAGE

See **thrust stage.**

ARAGOTO

(Japanese: ***Kabuki* theatre**.) A style of violent (melodramatic) acting developed by the *Kabuki* actor, Ichikawa Danjuro I (1660-1704). A style suited to the *samurai* (warrior) roles of historical romances, *aragoto* simply exaggerated the costumes, makeup, gestures and speech of the warrior class, thus transposing the action from the present into the fictional past. (A juvenile analogy to the entrance of the *Kabuki* actor in the *aragoto* style would be the arrival of the Lone Ranger in the nick of time to challenge the bad guys).

(See Earle Ernst, *The Kabuki Theatre*, 1956.)

ARCHETYPE

Literally, the original, from which all of its kind are descended; archetypes in literature and drama, and by extension the rest of the arts, link specific works to the characters, themes, structures and images of generic tradition. Cartoon or T.V. depictions of the Lone Ranger, for example, are "archetypal images" which relate the Lone Ranger to the long tradition of heroic horsemen depicted in painting, sculpture and literature. Similarly, paintings and sculptures of St. George and the Dragon relate back to the dim history of horseman heroes and forward to the Lone Ranger. The component parts of the image (hero, horse, weapon, **sidekick** and damsel-in-distress) constitute a syntactical pattern of signs reinterpreted countless times. From this point of view, every work of art has two complementary dimensions of meaning: the **synchronic**, in which the work is a unique creation in the context of its own time and **diachronic,** in which the work is part of a tradition. This is the paradox of artistic creation: from one point of view, each work is unique; from another, there is nothing new under the sun.

It has been noted that various dramatic **genres** have archetypal structures: comedies are about young men and women overcoming obstacles to their union from the older generation and so on. Similarly, comic characters, such as the avaricious old man, the braggart soldier, the tricky slave and others are archetypal characters, who are freshly reinterpreted with each new comedy. Domestic comedies tend to hinge upon money--often in the form of inheritances--because money is a symbol of social power; comedies end with weddings or banquets or some form of celebration, because comedy is about fertility; comedies derive their fun from the ridicule of the icons of social sterility (usually the older generation or the establishment).

(See especially Northrop Frye, *Anatomy of Criticism*, 1958.)

ARENA STAGE

A type of theatrical space, such as the classical Greek theatre, in which the audience surrounds most, if not all of the performance space. This definition reminds us that events such as football games are inherently theatrical (see **theatre**).

ARIA

(Italian) A closed form of sung speech for the solo performer in opera, the aria's dramaturgical function is similar to that of the dramatic soliloquy in that it allows the expression of the private feelings and thoughts of a character. It is for this reason that the aria is self contained musically and poetically, whereas **recitative** is a musical form of on-going dialogue.

ARIOSO

(Italian) A form of sung speech mid way between **aria** and **recitative**: more lyrical and expressive than recitative, but not a closed form like an aria.

ARLECCHINO

A **commedia dell'arte** stock character (masked) of the _zanni_, or servant class. Known cross culturally as the "**trickster**" figure (Jung's trickster archetype), Arlecchino, or Harlequin in England, was a wiley servant of gross physical and sexual appetites, usually dressed in patches.

The Trickster is essentially a farce **archetype**, imported into **comedy** as an aide to the hero in his attempt to break the bondage of the older generation. In some commedia scenarios, the Trickster figure becomes the centre of the action, thus shifting the play toward farce.

ART FOR ART'S SAKE

A movement in Europe (also known as "aestheticism") which attempted to refocus the function of art, from social utility (e.g., "to entertain and teach") and mere representation to self justified, internally self sufficient expressions of "the beautiful." Art was viewed as an end in itself, not as a means to an end (and especially not a means to some patron's end). If art has a **social function**, it is to serve as an antidote to Western science, technology and materialism. The movement, in England, was led by a group of "decadents," who were also involved in the "art nouveau" movement (which in turn was related to the "arts and crafts" movement and the "pre-Raphaelites") and included Walter Pater, Oscar Wilde, Aubrey Beardsley, W.B. Yeats, and William Morris. In its extreme form, the movement was a decadent romanticism in which the borderline between art and life was deliberately blurred. The movement was satirized in Gilbert and Sullivan's _Patience_, 1881. In France, _l'art pour l'art_ was a cry for an autonomous art and spontaneous creativity and included a variety of artists such as Baudelaire, Verlaine and Huysmans. (See **modernism**.)

(See Oscar Wilde, *The Decay of Lying*, 1889; Jose Ortega y Gasset, *The Dehumanization of Art*, 1925.)

ASIDE

A dramaturgical code / theatrical **convention** whereby the private thoughts of a character can be heard by the audience (through direct address), but not by the others on stage. The aside was used heavily in 19th century melodrama to facilitate the communication of the villain's plans and self-justifications. With the advent of **realism**, the aside had to be sublimated (or more accurately **displaced**) to be acceptable: the result was **subtext**, or the implied thoughts/feelings/intentions of a character embedded in the dialogue.

AUDIENCE

One element of the **performance triad**, a three cornered dramaturgical relationship between the performer(s), the text and the audience. The audience metaphorically represents "the community" for whom the **ritual** is being enacted, but since both parties are present by mutual consent (see **theatre**), the performers are part of that community. All communities have two fundamental, interacting dimensions: the individual and the collective. Since each member of the audience decodes signs produced by the actors, director, designer and playwright according to personal as well as communal and cultural predispositions, he or she modifies the collective interpretation of the event.

(See also Susan Bennett, *Theatre Audiences: a Theory of Production and Reception* (London: Routledge, 1990.)

AUDITORIUM

(Latin: "hearing place.) The etymology of the term suggests a change in perspective between Roman and Greek theatre (see *theatron*, "seeing place") from an emphasis on the visual code system to an emphasis on the aural. In practical terms this may have reflected the difference between the preponderance of choral dancing in archaic Greek theatre and Roman rhetoric.

AUTO SACREMENTAL

(Spanish: "work from the sacrament.") A one act verse play associated with the Feast of Corpus Christi in medieval and Renaissance Spanish drama. (See, e.g., Calderon's *The Great World Theatre*, 1645.)

AVANT GARDE

(French: "advance guard" or "vanguard".) A term which refers specifically to a radical shift in all of the arts from the middle of the 19th century, marking a social as well as an artistic break between the "establishment" (from academy to bourgeois gallery) and commercialism, on the one hand, and the revolutionaries on the other. The culmination of tendencies within **Romanticism**, the avant garde led the way to **modernism** in both radical subject matter and innovative forms. Most avant garde activity in the theatre at this time found outlets in the independent theatre movement which swept Europe (Theatre Libre, Theatre de l'Oeuvre, Independent Theatre, Die Freie Buhne, Abbey Theatre, Moscow Art Theatre). The following list includes the major avant garde movements associated with theatre during the turn of the century (all terms are discussed elsewhere in the *Dictionary*):

SYMBOLISM	(1885-1910, France)
EXPRESSIONISM	(1900-1920's, Germany)
FUTURISM	(1908-1930, Italy)
DADAISM	(1916-1920, Switzerland)
CONSTRUCTIVISM	(1912-1920's, Russia)
SURREALISM	(1924-1930, France)
EPIC THEATRE	(1920--. Germany)
MODERNISM	(1945--)
POST MODERNISM	(1965--)

B

BALLAD OPERA

An 18th century English parody of Italian opera, the ballad opera was popular, had spoken dialogue and featured original lyrics set to existing popular songs. The content of the ballad opera was satirical and often aimed at the political and social foibles of the day--ultimately leading to increased censorship (such as the Licensing Act of 1737). The ballad opera was also a major precursor of the **operetta** and **musical comedy**. (See John Gay's *The Beggar's Opera*, 1728, and the theatrical prints of William Hogarth.)

BALLET DE COUR

(See **figure 12.**) The French form of courtly entertainment during the Renaissance which incorporated music, dance and scenic spectacle--all usually involving allegorical representations and complex **iconography**--in a celebratory text written in verse. (See also **intermezzo, masque.)**

Possibly the most elaborate of the *ballet de cour*, and certainly the most complex, the *Ballet Comique de la Reyne* (1581), was staged by French humanists for the embattled court of Henry IV. Ostensibly in honour of a court favourite (the Duc de Joyeuse), the ballet was actually intended to gain political support for the monarchy in its current religious quarrels.

(See Frances Yates, *Astraea: the Imperial Theme in the 16th Century*, 1975.)

BAROQUE

An art historical term referring roughly to the 17th century, but depending on geographical location, beginning as early as the mid 16th century and lasting through the early 18th in a style called "rococo." (See **figure 13: "Periodicity."**)

Strictly speaking, baroque refers to a theatrical and emotional consciousness in the design of an architectural space, a consciousness which extends to the elaborate ornamentation in a building's sculptural and painted decorations. Probably the greatest example of "high baroque" in this sense is St. Peter's in Rome, but many major monuments exist in other countries: much of Louis XIV's Versailles and the Whitehall Banqueting House of James I are baroque, for example.

In music, the baroque refers to a similar theatrical consciousness and ornamentation, as exemplified by the development of **opera** and later by the oratorios of Bach and Handel.

In non musical theatre, **neoclassicism** held sway through this period, but the **heroic tragedies** of the Restoration period in England and even the tragedies of Corneille in France are particularly "baroque" in consciousness. So too are the sentiments of Shakespeare in such lines as "all the world's a stage" and "the poor player who struts and frets his life upon the stage." Inigo Jones' elaborate visual allegories designed for Ben Jonson's court masques were influenced by Italian baroque sculpture and architecture.

In terms of **social function**, the baroque is the artistic expression of absolutism and the "hey day" of the equestrian aristocracy, but it also became the style of the Counter Reformation in the art and architecture of the Catholic church.

(See Manfred F. Bukofzer, *Music in the Baroque Era*, 1947; Frank J. Warnke, *Versions of the Baroque: Euopean Literature in the 17th Century*, 1972; Roy Strong, *Splendour at Court: Renaissance Spectacle and Illusion*, 1973; Judith Hook, *The Baroque Age in England,* 1976.)

BAUHAUS

A revolutionary interdisciplinary school of the arts in Germany (c. 1920's &

'30's) with principle centres in Weimar and Dessau. Led by such **avant garde** artists as Walter Gropius, Laszlo Moholy-Nagy and Kandinsky, the Bauhaus flourished as the German manifestation of the international Arts and Crafts movement with its socialist connections. The basic philosophy which guided Gropius through most of the school's history was that modern design and technology should not lose touch with their roots in the crafts, nor should there be a division between fine and applied arts. Also influential in the school, in terms of classes, faculty and public events was the desire to bring all of the arts under one roof for their mutual benefit and for the cross fertilization of ideas and techniques (**synergy**).

The performing arts branch of the school, while secondary to that of the visual arts, was led by Oskar Schlemmer (*Triadic Ballet*, 1923) and Kurt Schmidt (*The Mechanical Cabaret*, 1923).

(See Marcel Franciscono, *Walter Gropius and the Creation of the Bauhaus at Weimar*, 1971; H.M. Wingler, *The Bauhaus*, 1969; Walter Gropius, ed., *The Theatre of the Bauhaus*, 1961.)

BEAT

A term coined in American versions of the Stanislavski system of acting (the **method**), "beats" are the internal structural units of **french scenes** in terms of **feedback loops** (initiative/response/adjustment); a unit of **action** limited by the specific sub objectives of engaged characters: when the objective changes, a new beat begins. Theoretically, actors (as characters) focus on successive sub objectives while pursuing "super objectives" just as a downhill skier focuses on each gate enroute to victory.[9]

BIO-MECHANICS

Vsevolod Meryerhold (1874-1940), Russian Director, student/colleague of Stanislavsky used this term to characterize his attempts to foreground or prioritise the

---

[9]Robert Cohen, *Acting Power* (Davis: Mayfield, 1979), p.86.

kinetic **code system** in actor training and performance. Bio-mechanics begins with the theory that all truth begins in the nervous system, not in the **"emotional memory.** In **reception theory**, this notion substitutes empathy for sympathy in audience response to stage action--the vicarious reaction to the kinetic dimension *precedes* the emotional identification with characters.

In actor training, Meyerhold emphasized physical work: rhythm, coordination, reflexes, the body in space/time etc. (which led to **constructivism** in staging and set design). The result of such training led to a dancer's interpretation of the text and a highly kinetic performance.

(See Robert Leach, *Vsevolod Meryerhold*, 1989; James M. Symons, *Meyerhold's Theatre of the Grotesque*, 1971.)

BLANK VERSE

A line of unrhymed verse written in iambic pentameter; blank verse is particularly suited to dramatic speeches and dialogue in that the meter is freely spoken. Blank verse is the unsung equivalent of **recitative** in opera.

BLOCKING

This refers to planned movement on the stage: "utility blocking" is the simple, but essential process of organizing entrances and exits, required crosses and seating; "organic blocking" is the more complex and personal movement governed by character **objectives**, relationships and conflicts; "patterned blocking" is the sense of artistic unity and design imparted to all stage movement by the director, which provide flow, tempo, variety and rhythm to connected stage pictures.

Movement is kinetic communication; it is powerful, but "primitive," in that its appeal is vicarious and usually unconscious. In the hierarchy of the **multi-modal communication system**, movement can overpower visual and especially aural messages--hence traditional rules of thumb, such as, "when you move, don't speak," or, "don't move on another's lines"--rules which can be ignored for special effect.

(See Raymond Birdwhistle, *Introduction to Kinesics*, 1957; Frank P. Jones, *Body Awareness in Acting*, 1976; Arthur Lessac, *Body Wisdom: The Use and Training of the Body*, 1978.)

There are many texts on directing. Three relatively recent ones with significant chapters on blocking are: Robert Cohen & John Harrop, *Creative Play Direction*, 2nd edition, 1984; Francis Hodge, *Play Directing*, 3rd edition, 1988; Louis E. Catron, *The Director's Vision*, 1989).

BOMOLOCHUS

(Greek: "buffoon") The buffoon role type cited as one of three types of comic character in the Roman MS *Tractatus Coislinianus*, a recod of classical types. (See also, *alazon* and *eiron*.)

BOURGEOIS TRAGEDY

Tragedy involving middle class characters as central agents of the **action.** In his preface to *The London Merchant* (1731), George Lillo defended this shift from traditional **tragedy** on the grounds that dramatic actions concerning the lives of the nobility were not sufficiently applicable to the lives of the majority of citizens (or the majority of his audiences), but that the principles and thus the moral lessons to be learned were the same.[10] This was a plea for social relevance with far reaching dramaturgical, as well as commercial, consequences (see **melodrama, drame, thesis play** and the **well-made play**).

In terms of **social function**, bourgeois tragedy was an indicator of both the rise of the middle class to economic and political power and its emulation (envy) of the cultural symbols and forms of the class it was replacing. In economic terms, the middle class and its tastes simply ruled the box office.

---

[10]George Lillo, *The London Merchant: Dedication*. From Dougald MacMillan and Howard M. Jones, *Plays of the Restoration and Eighteenth Century* (New York: Holt, Rinehardt and Winston, 1931), pp. 617-18.

BOX

A type of theatre seating: "box seats" were the most expensive seats in a type of auditorium divided by social class. In other words, ticket prices reinforced features of theatre architecture: "box, **pit** and **gallery**." Instituted in the Drury Lane and other London theatres of the late 18th century, box seats were a bi-product of middle class commercial theatre.

(See James J. Lynch, *Box, Pit and Gallery: Stage and Society in Johnson's London* (Berkeley: University of California Press, 1953.)

BOX SET

Stage settings of interiors with three complete walls gradually replaced the "wing and drop" system through the first half of the 18th century. For example, Madame Vestris is generally credited with introducing the box set into England in the 1830's. A box set meant that entrances had to be made through doors, that furnishings became obstacle courses for **blocking** and that the **"fourth wall"** convention, reinforced by a strong proscenium arch and little or no forestage, would complete the movement toward **realism** and **representational theatre**. The box set was also an indication of the growing influence of the middle class on the dramaturgy of theatre and drama: the new audience favoured believable reproductions of their own domestic surroundings.

BUNRAKU

The Japanese doll theatre (a.k.a. "*Joruri*" and "*Gidayu-bushi*") of the 17th and 18th centuries. The *Bunraku* was a popular form of theatre involving large, hand manipulated puppets, instrumental accompanyment (on the *samisen*) and spoken narrative (by a chanter). Stories were adapted from popular fiction and historical romances, especially by Chikamatsu Monzaemon (1653-1724); and the form of the presentation was perfected by the chanter, Takemoto-Gidayu (1650-1714). The puppet handlers were visible in some versions, although dressed in black and by convention, invisible. This dramaturgical feature, plus the combination of the narrative past and the dramatic present gave the *Bunraku* its complex appeal (see also **Noh**). Once it became commercially popular, the style was imitated by **Kabuki** actors.

(See Donald Keene, *Bunraku: the Art of Japanese Puppet Theatre*, 1965.)

BURLESQUE

(Italian: *burlesco*, "mocking") In the 17th century a burlesque was a full length parody of a well known play or style (in the sense that John Gay's *Beggar's Opera_*"burlesques" Italian Opera). Other examples include *The Rehearsal*, by George Villiers and Sheridan's *The Critic*.

In the 19th century, in England, the burlesque degenerated into simple music hall entertainments which heaped ridicule on current fashions, while in America the burlesque ("burleycue") became a variety show framed by chorus lines of female dancers. Aimed principally at a working class male audience, the burleycue was a low form of entertainment filled with parodies, jokes and finally striptease. The late forms of burlesque were practically indistinguishable from the "extravaganza," the "harliquinade" and the "pantomime" (in England) except perhaps in the relative degree of spectacle. In short, these terms had more to do with advertising than artistic form or content. Nevertheless, they all kept live theatre before a popular audience and elements found their way into major forms, such as musical comedy.

(See R. Wilmuth, *Kindly Leave the Stage*, 1992; see also **Vaudeville**.)

BURLETTA

At first a type of comic opera imported into England in the latter part of the 18th century, the *burletta* became a means of circumventing the regulations of the Licencing Act and the Lord Chamberlain's office. A company could perform regular plays if they had no more than three acts and each contained at least five songs. Robert Elliston, **actor-manager** of the Surrey Theatre in 1809, thus transformed *Macbeth* into a song and dance "tragedy."[11]

BUSINESS

Business includes small scale activities, such as lighting a cigarette, which an actor builds into the development of the physical character to help illustrate sub-textual life and psychological peculiarities and to create a sense of a total "persona." Since all such activity is part of the performance as a **multi-modal communication system**, business must be used judiciously and organically, lest it be superficial, misleading and/or distracting. (See also **mask**.)

---

[11]Oscar Brockett, *History of the Theatre*, 6th edition (New York: Allyn and Bacon, 1991), p. 460.

C

CABARET

Generally, an intimate theatrical space which also serves food and drink to the audience during various kinds of performances, from musical groups to plays; a nightclub. Cabaret theatre became particularly popular for **avant garde** and "decadent" entertainment in Germany between the wars. The heyday of the French equivalent was the cafe society of *la belle epoche* in Paris (ca. 1890-1920); in America nightclubs flourished through the Prohibition eara to the Drepression.

CAPITANO

A stock character from the ***commedia dell'arte*** of the ***miles gloriosus*** or "braggart warrior" type (see ***alazon***). Capitano is usually an ally of ***Pantalone*** and a sexual competitor of the hero.

CATASTROPHE

(Greek: *katastrophe*, "overturning") The point in the **plot** of a play when the result of the **action** occurs: e.g., when Oedipus appears, blinded, before the chorus; in comedy, when the last piece of the puzzle is revealled and the "old society" is defeated (see **Freytag's Pyramid, dramatic structure, plot**).

CATHARSIS

(Greek: *katharsis*, "to purge") From Aristotle's *Poetics*, the term applies to the effect of **tragedy** on the audience, and is thus a concern of **reception theory**. To

Aristotle it might have meant purging in the sense of getting rid of the emotions created by the tragic **action** and leaving the spectator cleansed; or it might have meant purging in the sense that the action purged the "sickness" the spectator brought with him to the theatre (i.e., by dealing with hidden fears in a symbolic ritual).

In any case, the concept has profound implications for the ritual origins and fundamental nature of the theatrical event. In this regard, the investigations of Claude Levi-Strauss into shamanic ritual in which the curative powers of the "group abreaction" are similar to the function of catharsis.[12] Simply stated, the Shaman cures his patient of disease by travelling to the nether world to battle with and/or trick the evil forces responsible. This **performance**, accompanied by drum and dance and other business, is conducted *in a context of belief*: the patient and the gathered community understand and believe in the process and in the ability of the Shaman/actor to heal.

Similarly, while the theatrical event usually has an immediate **social function** related to the patronage structures of the particular time and place, it also has an underlying *communal* function concerned with the cohesion (and health) of the community which is reinforced by the act of coming together, physically and emotionally, and sharing a cultural tradition. In this sense, catharsis is by no means limited to tragedy (or even **drama**).

Erwin Panofsky has suggested a parallel function in the visual arts in his analysis of the shepherds' reaction to the Christ Child in Hugo van der Goes' *Portinari Altarpiece* as one of "elation and terror in the contemplation of the sublime."[13]

---

[12]Claude Levi-Strauss, *Structural Anthropology*, translated by Claire Jacobson and Brooke Grundfest Schoepf (New York: Basic Books, 1963), p. 181.

[13]Erwin Panofsky, *Early Netherlandish Painting, its Origins and Character*, vol. 1 (New York: Harper and Row, 1971, 1953), p. 332.

CHAMBER PLAY

A modern form conceived and promoted by August Strindberg (see his *Preface to Miss Julie*, 1888). The idea of the chamber play (and the small theatres in which they would be produced, such as Max Reinhardt's *Kammerspiel*) was a logical offshoot of the dramaturgy of **realism**: a need for more intimacy between audience and stage and a desire to avoid the illusion breaking intermissions of longer plays. The short form, with the relatively small cast, was cheaper to produce and more conducive to experiment and the treatment of radical ideas. From this point of view, Strindberg's chamber plays were the true ancestors of modern **alternative theatre**. (See also: **music theatre**.)

CHARACTER

(Persona/mask) Plays involve fictional people who engage each other in the pursuit of personal **objectives**. Characters and what they do are the fundamental elements of **dramaturgy**, i.e., the writer's most important control is over the characters he chooses to be in his play--their number, age, sex, occupation and so on.

To Aristotle, characters are the primary **agents** of the **action** of a play: "character" is not so much an abstract essence (in the sense of moral fibre or personality), but a *quality which reveals purpose*: characters *are* what characters *do*.[14] From this perspective, we become acquainted with a character as the action progresses and we observe him making decisions or choices and acting on them. At the end, a character is the sum of all such choices and acts. What others say about him may not be relevant to our understanding of the character at all, but may reveal more about the person speaking. Similarly, we should never take what a character says about himself at face value: he may be lying, and the significance is in the lying, not in the lie (i.e., this is a character who lies).

Dramatic characters serve the playwright by fulfilling functions beyond

---

[14]Aristotle, *Poetics*, chap. 7, 1450a, 19-20.

themselves as individuals. They can be used archetypally as heroes and heroines, sidekicks and villains; they can personify or represent social forces or classes; or they can represent abstract ideas as in **morality plays** and **expressionist** drama--in every case, however, they are defined by what they do.

Since **drama** is fundamentally concerned with human relationships, the most revealing aspect of a character is his relationships with other characters and how he behaves toward them as he pursues his own **objectives**.

CHORUS

(Greek: "ring dancers") While the etymology of the word reminds us that the chorus was first of all a group of dancers and that the kinetic channel was important, in practice a chorus is a group of performers acting in concert and/or unison. The **Noh** chorus chants in unison, the *corps de ballet* often dances together and the Greek chorus did both, although there is some conjecture as to the degree of concert or the amount and places of unison.

The dramaturgical functions of a chorus can be many and varied. The Greek chorus, if we can take Sophocles' *Oedipus* as an illustration, is multi-functioned, and this complicates the dramaturgy of both text and performance. As a group, this chorus performs original, relevant, odes, thus adding the dimensions of music and dance to the dialogue. This in turn places the **issues** and thus the **action** of the play proper in a larger, more cosmic context. At the same time the chorus expresses its collective anxiety over the issues raised. In other words, the chorus places the **synchronic** issue in a **diachronic** context. The purpose of this is the preservation of a "living history:" issues of the day are given the weight of tradition.

While performing a choral ode, the chorus is usually alone on stage, expressing a collective idea to the only other collective present, the audience. At these points the performance is **presentational**. When the characters are on stage, however, the chorus is also present and neither acknowledges the existence of the audience, which means that the performance is temporarily **representational**.

In these scenes the chorus fulfills at least two other functions which affect the audience's perception of the characters' actions. Since it never leaves the stage, the chorus transforms what might have been private conversations (such as that between Oedipus and Tiresias) into public confrontations. The chorus thus serves as a silent witness to momentous events. Secondly, insofar as the chorus represents Athenian civilization, it represents that community on stage, and this makes the issues of the play important to the audience as citizens of the Greek state--the chorus speaks the public mind. (It is in this sense that a Greek tragedy is a *tribunal*.) In speaking for the audience, the chorus is more than a witness, but perhaps less than a character (a character is, and behaves, as an individual).

In all of its functions, then, the Greek chorus serves as an aesthetic bridge between the past and the present. In this instance *(Oedipus)* the major difference between the chorus and the audience is that the chorus does not share the audience's foreknowledge of events, which adds immeasurably to the **dramatic irony** of choral lines. The concurrent presence of chorus and characters thus makes a Greek tragedy a highly complex lesson in the history of dramaturgy.

(See T.B.L. Webster, *Greek Theatre Production*, 1970; Peter Arnott, *Greek Scenic Conventions in the 5th Century*, 1962 and *Public and Performance in the Greek Theatre*, 1989.)

CLASSICISM

Classicism in art criticism most commonly refers to qualities in later works which reflect those of the arts of ancient Greece and Rome. These qualities include a balanced coherence of parts-to-whole which is the hallmark of analytical thought. The classical impulse also restrains any tendency toward complications of forms, but gives highest priority to simplicity and intensity. (See also **neoclassicism**.)

In drama, classical tendencies are revealled in a causal structure, in a single **action**, and in a hierarchy of scenes of increasing intensity leading inevitably toward a **climax** and finally to a **resolution**--all of which give the work a sense of closure or completeness. In a classical play, all characters and events are directly related to the central action. Such a play thus reveals the Greek sense of reason in its very structure.

CLIMAX

(Greek: *klimax*, "ladder") The apex in the crisis of a scene or play as a whole. In traditional dramaturgy, the climax comes near the end of a scene or play, which means that it is preceded by a **rising action** and followed by a falling action or **denouement**. An "anti-climax" is thus a scene or moment which is less than expected at that point in the action, or an event which detracts from the true climax.

CLOWN

A character/performer who exhibits totally unjustified total confidence and "triumph in the face of adversity;" or one who is "the eternal optimitst," or one who could be defined as "human pretention, punctured with a grin." Although we tend to associate clowns specifically with the circus, they have been a part of other forms of theatre from ancient times. (See **fool, trickster.**)

CODE SYSTEM

A dramatic text and a theatrical performance communicate by means of interacting code or sign systems through three basic channels: aural, visual and kinetic (or sound, image and movement). In the dramatic text, these codes are **embedded** in the dialogue with references to movement, **off-stage life, properties,** sounds and any other dramaturgical element. The following hypothetical lines demonstrate some of these codes:

> "Listen to me! I want you to take this gun, go through the kitchen door--make sure you slam it--and shoot the first person you see. When I hear the shot, I'll phone the police."

Directors, actors, designers and choreographers interpret these codes and "translate" them into **performance** codes for an audience (which, in turn, decodes them--see

reception theory). In the above lines there are references to props (gun and telephone), movement, sounds and off-stage life (which will affect on-stage life). Depending on their context within the play and the interpretations given them by the actors and director, these lines could be from a psychological thriller or a grotesque farce.

(See Elaine Ashton and George Savona, *Theatre as a Sign System: a Semiotics of Text and Performance*, 1991; Kier Elam, *The Semiotics of Theatre and Drama*, 1980.)

COLLECTIVE CREATION

Referring as much to a *process* as a *product*, collective creations are a genre of the **alternative theatre** movement. The process involves all members of the creative team--actors, director(s), writer(s), designer(s) and even technicians--in a method of play creation which begins with an idea and procedes through a period of research (whether empirical or documentary) to improvisation and discussion, from rough drafts to rehearsal and revision and finally to performance. One of the objectives behind this process has been to subvert the traditional hierarchy of play production (writer>>director>>actor) and substitute a collective energy and creativity. In practice there has been a tension between this more democratic method and the efficiency and focus of an individual director or writer.

(See Renate Usmiani, *Second Stage The Alternative Theatre Movment in Canada,* 1983; Alan Filewod, *Collective Encounters: Documentary Theatre in English Canada,* 1987; T. Shank, *American Alternative Theatre*, 1982.)

COLUMBINA

A *commedia dell'arte* (masked) character, *Zanni* class; confidante to the heroine; a female **trickster** in love with *Arlecchino*; the English Columbine.

COMEDY

(See **figure 1: "The Ur Drama, Spring"**) Traditionally, one of the two principle dramatic genres (see **tragedy**), comedy is an **action** which celebrates community renewal through the victory of a hero and/or heroine over representatives of an "old society." This view, analysed in detail by Northrop Frye,[15] is a generic description of male dominated traditional theatre. Feminist criticism, however, re-orients the discussion.[16] The **archetypal** comic structure generally proceeds as follows:

> --*From* a state of bondage, in which the old society holds the power (of inheritance, marriage, money, tradition, livelihood, etc.) to control the lives of the younger generation;
> --*through* a period of struggle between the young and old, in which the young are aided by a **trickster** figure;
> --*to* the celebration of the hero's victory (with a wedding and/or feast, which implies the "birth" of a new society).

A number of comments should be made about this archetypal pattern:

> 1. the process reaffirms the norms of the larger community, which includes the audience;
>
> 2. comedy, according to Northrop Frye, is the polar opposite of **tragedy** and as such is a **displaced** ritual of renewal;[17]
>
> 3. the pattern also bears a strong resemblance to a "rite of passage," in which adolescents are tested before being accepted into adult society;[18]
>
> 4. the strong presence of slaves, servants and/or persons of a lower social class, who are both the cause and objects of humour, means that the theme of bondage versus freedom is often repeated at different levels of society;
>
> 5. individual comedies may focus on a single phase of the pattern, with the happy ending merely implied;

---

[15]Frye, *Anatomy of Criticism: Four Essays* (Princeton: Princeton University Press, 1957).

[16]Susan Carlson, *Women and Comedy: Re-writing the British Theatrical Tradition* (Ann Arbor: University of Michigan Press, 1991).

[17]Frye, *Anatomy of Criticism*, Third Essay: "Archetypal Criticism."

[18]Arnold van Gennep, *The Rites of Passage*, translated by Monika B. Vizedom and Gabrielle L. Caffee (Chicago: Chicago Univ. Press, 1969).

6. the **social function** of comedy is achieved through trickery and through the ridicule of inappropriate behaviour, and these events are comedy's chief sources of humour;

7. comedy, while employing elements of the farcical to achieve its ends, should be clearly distinguished from **tragicomedy** and **farce** on one hand, and **melodrama** on the other.

Other theories of comedy focus on different aspects of the genre such as the laughter produced by comedies--that is, the sources, effects and purpose of laughter--comic characters; comic themes, and so on.

(See also: Susan K. Langer, *Feeling and Form*, 1963; Henri Bergson, "Laughter," in *Comedy*, Wylie Sypher, ed., 1956).

COMEDY OF HUMORS, MANNERS AND WIT

These are sub types of the comic genre, generally associated with specific historical periods and/or societies. The comedy of humors is based on the psycho-physical notions of behaviour in the Renaissance: i.e., one's behaviour is dictated by the balance of bodily fluids or "humors;" when these are out of balance, one exhibits extreme behaviour, which must be corrected. (See the comedies of Ben Jonson, such as *Everyman in his Humor*, 1598.)

The comedy of manners places its focus on the manners of an elite, fashionable class, to which the hero and heroine belong and intend to reform. While comedies of manners are found in several historical periods, they are most prevalent in those where there are economic and political shifts in power, as from the aristocracy of the 18th century to the middle-class of the 19th century. (See the comedies of Moliere, Congreve, Sheridan, Wilde and Coward.)

A comedy of "wit" is a sub category of the comedy of manners in that it refers specifically to those plays of the English Restoration period (and possibly Oscar Wilde) in which the most prized "weapon of choice" in social intercourse is fashionable wit. In these comedies, those with "true wit" defeat pretenders or "would wits."

(See Thomas Hobbes, *Leviathan*, 1651; Thomas H. Fujimura, *The Restoration Comedy of Wit*, 1952.)

COMIC RELIEF

Against the rules of **neoclassicism**, scenes of comic relief in a serious play or tragedy, such as the gravediggers' scene in *Hamlet*, provide an ironic perspective on the tragic action. At the same time, and as the term implies, these scenes interrupt the relentless tragic rhythm and thereby allow it to grow to even greater levels of intensity. Scenes of comic releif were the dramaturgical precursors of modern **tragicomedy**.

COMMEDIA DELL'ARTE

Italian professional comedy which flourished through the 16th and 17th centuries. The form was characterized by partially improvised performances, professional actors and companies and stock characters. Improvised dialogue, based on **scenarios** written for specific actors and companies, was supplemented with *lazzi*, or memorized comic routines--everything from a song or pompous speech to slapstick physical routines. Most successful actors had a repertoire of appropriate lazzi which became their trademarks. As companies became successful through appearances at the various courts of Europe, the improvised nature of their routines declined and commedia troupes began to lose touch with their roots.

Professional actors of the commedia, many inventing and perfecting one character throughout their careers, kept the profession and its close connection with paying audiences alive during centuries dominated by court patronage. Companies, such as the I Gelosi (1570's to 1604), were known and sought after throughout the courts of Europe. Led by Flamino Scala (poet, nobleman, actor), Francesco Andreini (actor) and Isabella Andreini (poet, singer, actress), the I Gelosi perfected many of the characters and routines which have come down to the present time through the works of later playwrights.

Stock characters of the commedia were divided into three social groups: the hero and heroine, the middle-class, and the servants. The first, with names such as "Lillio" and "Isabella" were unmasked, and thus more "human;" the second, represented by **Pantalone** and **Capitano**, were masked, and the third (***Zanni***), represented by **Arlecchino** and **Columino**, were also masked.

Scenarios, which contained outlines of plots, lists of characters, entrances and exits (**french scenes**), places for lazzi, typically focused on the schemes and tricks of the servants in their often bumbling attempts to thwart their masters (usually in aid of the lovers). Many of these scenarios have survived and are available in translation.[19] (See Pierre L. Duchartre, *The Italian Comedy*, 1929; G. Oreglia, *The Commedia dell'arte*, 1968; John Rudlin, *Commedia Dell'Arte: An Actor's Handbook*, 1992.)

COMMEDIA ERUDITA

(Italian: "learned comedy") Originally amateur and related to the humanist academies, these comedies attempted to imitate ancient plays, especially those of Plautus and Terrence. They were performed in the academies and at court; they were written (as opposed to being improvised) and they abided by the "rules" of **neoclassicism**.

COMPLICATION

In traditional dramaturgy, this is the development section of the **plot**, where the **issues** and characters introduced develop in complexity. This section is usually the longest in the play. (See **Freytag's Pyramid.**)

CONFIDANTE

Although this character can be either male or female, in drama she is usually

---

[19]Henry E. Salerno, translator and editor, *Scenarios of the Commedia dell'Arte: Flaminio Scala's Il Teatro Delle Favole Rappresentative* (New York: Proscenium Publishers, 1992).

the heroine's "sidekick:" a person of lower rank in whom the heroine can confide; also, a person whose lower rank (or race) provides opportunities to aid the heroine in circumventing the restrictions of parents, guardians or society in general. The confidante may assume many roles, from Juliet's Nurse in *Romeo and Juliet* to Laurey's friend, Ado Annie, in *Oklahoma!*. Traditionally, the *confidante* (again for reasons of social class) is more earthy than the heroine and provides much of a comedy's sexual humour.

Dramaturgically, the *confidante* functions to facilitate the revelation of the heroine's thoughts and feelings through dialogue (as opposed to **soliloquy or monologue**)--a function which became less important with the development of **subtext**.

CONSTRUCTIVISM

A **modernist** style of staging and stage design which developed out of the collage in the visual arts; also, a post-revolutionary Russian movement pioneered by Vladimir Tatlin (1885-1956) and others in the visual arts and adapted for the theatre by Meyerhold.

In the theatre, the movement influenced the development of abstract "acting machines" composed of ramps, staircases, scaffolding and trapezes which would aid performers' physical creativity and facilitate directors' non-literal staging. Constructivist techniques, coupled with **bio-mechanics** and the theories of Adolphe Appia, led to experiments with **expressionist** drama and to innovative interpretations such as Peter Brook's *A Midsummer Night's Dream*, 1970.

(See Edward Braun, *Meyerhold on Theatre*, 1969.)

CONFLICT

See *agon* and **drama**

CONVENTION

A mutually understood usage of a theatrical **code system**, between the producers (playwright, director, designers, and/or actors) and receivers (the audience); the "rules of the game." There are acting conventions, staging conventions and social conventions (which may apply to the "society" on stage or to the audience or to both).

Conventions have been both traditional (i.e., maintained within specific cultures over time) and innovative (i.e., "invented" by one of the producers for a specific play or performance). In the latter case, the directions needed to understand the convention are embedded in either the text or the performance, or both.

The **proscenium arch**, for example, originally an architectural feature used to hide the machinery of perspective scenery, soon became a *frame*, placing the stage "picture" in perspective by creating **aesthetic distance**. The resulting *illusion* became a convention of the performance: it was understood that everything on the stage side of the arch constituted a separate reality. Part of this convention, therefore, dictated that the frame could not be "broken" by a performer through direct address without breaking the convention.

Other common conventions include the **soliloquy, aside, monologue** and even **impersonation**. Most conventions in the theatre, as "rules of the game," require a "willing suspension of disbelief."[20]

CORYPHAEUS

(Greek: "head" or "foremost") The leader of the Greek **chorus**; the most prominent (and representative) position on stage; the actor who speaks individual lines (as opposed to choral odes spoken/sung and/or chanted in unison). (Cf: *choregus*, the sponsor of a production.)

---

[20]S.T. Coleridge, "Progress of the Drama," in Dukore *Dramatic Theory and Criticism*, p. 587.

COSTUME

A costume is a visual code; it helps identify and define a character in terms of age, sex, class, occupation, dramatic function, personal taste and even subtextual attitude. A costume is thus a systemic overlay of visual information, but the "meaning" of a specific costume is only clear in the context of the character in his/her *relationships* ("we dress for others"). A white wedding gown is one thing; the same gown on a wicked witch is quite another.

CRISIS

See **drama** and **agon**.

CROSS DRESSING

Gender illusions created by actors playing the opposite sex. Many theatrical traditions have highly developed forms of cross dressing, from the female impersonators on the British and American night club circuit to the **Kabuki** *Onagata*. Shakespeare, writing women's roles for a theatrical tradition which did not permit female actors, was a master at creating characters who "cross dressed," thereby reverting to the actor's real gender. Viola, in *Twelfth Night* and Rosalind in *As You Like It*, for example, both play "breeches parts:" that is, both of these female roles are played by young male actors who adopt male disguises.

CROWD

(E.g., "crowd scene") If **duets, trios** and **quartets** have specific dramaturgical functions and characteristics, so does a crowd scene. Unless five or more people are distinctly blocked as smaller combinations (e.g., a duet and a trio), a crowd is five or more people on stage at the same time.

Crowds on stage are most often employed dramaturgically to place the action of a duet or trio in a "public" context--the crowd is employed as a background to the foregrounded dialogue. The prototype of the crowd is the **Greek chorus.** The 19th century Duke of Saxe Meiningen and his stage manager, Ludwig Chronegh, revolutionized the staging of crowd scenes by making each member a distinct personality engaged in the action and by blocking the crowd in more natural groups, each with a leader.

(See Max Grube, *The Story of the Meiningen*, 1963.)

D

DADA

As a **code** word, *dada* signals anarchy (dadadadada). In theatre, art and music Dada was a **modernist**, WWI movement in Europe (especially Switzerland), influenced by Italian **Futurism** and inspired by the work of Alfred Jarry. The Dadaists were part of the radical avant garde / alternative theatre which rejected most of the fundamentals of traditional art and dramaturgy, and the social values which produced them. They subjected their works and audiences to elements of anarchy (see **farce**) and chance as a symbolic protest against a society which had lost all reason in its pursuit of empire through war. To the Dadaists, western "radicalism" had forfeited all legitimacy.

Dada was an offshoot of 19th century **romanticism** in both its rebellion against traditional forms and in its pursuit of extreme subjectivity in art. In this respect, Dada soon became part of the **surrealist** movement in post war Europe. Dada re-emerged in the 1960's **fluxus** movement and in **happenings, environments** and ultimately in **performance art**. (See Maurice Nadeau, *The History of Surrealism*, 1965.)

DECONSTRUCTION

(See **post-structuralism, semiotics**.) A **post-modernist** critical strategy for exposing the fundamental ideological and aesthetic assumptions underlying works of art. Beginning with language, whose grammar betrays both cultural presuppositions and thought processes, this strategy considers all structures of sign systems to be culturally "contaminated." Deconstruction thus looks beyond the work to the creative *process* of artistic consciousness in both performer and audience. The works of Richard Foreman, for example, *deconstruct* this consciousness, while such a play as *Lear* by Edward Bond deconstructs Shakespeare's text, exposing its hidden ideological assumptions.

It should be noted that most of the entries in this Dictionary are based on the principles and assumptions of traditional dramaturgy (but see **post modernism, performance theory**).

(See Jacques Derrida, *Writing and Difference*, 1978; Christopher Norris, *Deconstruction: Theory and Practice*, 1982; Jonathan Culler, *On Deconstruction*, 1984; Stratos E. Constantinidis, *Theatre Under Deconstruction? A Question of Approach* (New York: Garland, 1993).

DECORUM

(See **figure 9**) In **neoclassic theory**, decorum means conformity to the norms of social behaviour (in life and art): a character, for example, should behave according to the standards of gender, age, occupation and class. In comedy, deviations from decorum are ridiculed as when, in Congreve's *The Way of the World*, old Lady Wishfort attempts to behave as a young woman in her pursuit of "Sir Rowland."

Similarly, a play should observe the rules of dramaturgical decorum such as the **unities**, and **verisimilitude**; it should be written in an appropriate style ("high" for tragedy, "low" for comedy) and treat appropriate subjects and characters.

DENOUEMENT

(French: "to untie") If an action is complicated by its **plot**, the denouement, which follows the **climax**, brings it back to clarity; also, the final phase in a dramatic structure in which all loose ends are cleared up. (See **resolution, falling action**.)

DEIXIS

(Greek: "to show") Embedded linguistic codes which identify speakers, listeners and objects in the here and now (through personal pronouns and adverbs: "I, you;" "this, that;" "here, now.") Deixis defines the essence of live theatre: *presence:*

> Deixis . . . is what allows language an 'active' and dialogic function rather than a descriptive (narrative) and choric one: it is instituted at the origins of the drama as the necessary condition of a non-narrative form of world-creating discourse.[21]

DEUS EX MACHINA

(Latin: "god from the machine") (1) In Greek plays, a machine which would lower a god onto the stage (**production dramaturgy**); (2) in **textual dramaturgy**, a new character introduced late into the action to solve a problem (usually on behalf of the hero); (3) an artificial and unacceptable solution to the complication of the plot.

DEUTERAGONIST

(Greek: "second in the contest") The second actor in a play. The invention of the deuteragonist by Aeschylus in the early 5th century made **dialogue** possible, and thus the clash of **issues** through personal relationships (see **drama, tritagonist**).

DIACHRONIC

"Across time:" the analysis of a work in the context of its tradition. Archetypal criticism, for example, considers the diachronic dimension of a specific work. Significantly, all works of art are informed by two fundamental "dimensions:" the diachronic and the **synchronic**--the work in the context of its own time.

---

[21]Kier Elam, *The Semiotics of Theatre and Drama* (London: Methuen, 1980), p. 139.

DIALOGUE

(Greek: "conversation") Communication between characters through speech; in strict dramaturgical terms, the dialogue is the playwright's only vehicle to control the **code systems** of performance. Dialogue is the essence of **drama** (as opposed to **theatre**) in that it is the principle means of developing **issues** between characters.

DICTION

Aristotle pays more attention to diction than any other single element of tragedy.[22] By diction Aristotle refers to the parts of speech, their individual functions and their syntactical relations, the **style** of writing, and the delivery on the stage. In totality, therefore, he seems to subsume both diction and thought under **rhetoric**.

DIRECT ADDRESS

This occurs when an actor and/or a character addresses the audience directly from within the context of the play. This is a **convention** which does not necessarily destroy the illusion of actuality in the performance. That is, the person who addresses the audience may do so as a character or not, but always does so as a *performer*. (See **presentational theatre**.)

DISPLACEMENT

(See **figure 1: the "Ur Drama"**) This is a term borrowed from Northrop Frye's *Anatomy of Criticism:* "the adaptation of myth and metaphor to canons of morality and plausibility."[23] Displacement indicates the historical and social process whereby the archetypes of myth and ritual become the images, structures and conventions of poetry, fiction and drama: the **action of** *Oedipus*, for example, is a "displaced" scapegoat ritual. while Oedipus himself, as a legendary king, is the

---

[22]Aristotle. *Poetics*, chap. 20-22, 1456a, 20 - 1459b, 15.

[23]Frye, *Anatomy of Criticism*, p. 365.

displaced god. (See **musical comedy, opera** and **festive theatre** described as displaced festivals of renewal.)

DITHYRAMB

A Greek choral ode sung in honour of Dionysus; according to Aristotle, the form of festival performance from which tragedy evolved.[24]

DOCUMENTARY DRAMA

Most playscripts involve some research; documentary drama purports to be based on both research and documentation some of the dialogue is often taken verbatim from such documents as newspapers and magazines, diaries, trial transcripts, etc. The purpose is to dramatize historical events in a style which gives the impression of fact rather than fiction.

The **social function** of such theatre has often been to expose the "truth" behind events and thus to instruct the audience. Documentary drama and theatre had its origins in post revolutionary Russia (see Nikolay Evreinov's *The Storming of the Winter Palace*, 1920), but was much developed by the **Workers' Theatre** movement led by Erwin Piscator and Bertolt Brecht, who employed signs, film and slides to "document" their productions (see *lehrstuke*). **Epic Theatre** and the **Living Newspaper** were offshoots of their work.

(See Rolf Hochhuth's *The Deputy*, 1963; Joan Littlewood's *Oh What a Lovely War*, 1963; Peter Weiss's *The Investigation*, 1965; and Weiss's essay, "Materials and Models: Notes Toward a Definition of Documentary Theatre," 1968.)

DOMESTIC TRAGEDY

(See **bourgeois tragedy**) If we are to use this term specifically, it refers to melodramatic and sentimental "tragedies" about Elizabethan domestic strife such as *The Tragedy of Mr. Arden of Faversham* (anon., 1603). These plays functioned as

---

[24]Aristotle, *Poetics*, chap. 4, 1149a, 10.

popular cautionary tales derived from the medieval **morality play**, aimed at the education of the middle class.

DOTTORE

A **commedia dell'Arte** masked role: the quack doctor or academic, often in pursuit of the heroine, and an ally of **Pantalone.**

DOUBLE PLOT

(See **plot**) The first question is, can such a thing exist, or do we mean **sub plot**? Can a play have two sets of incidents, roughly equal in importance, running in parallel? Would such a structure involve two **actions**? If this is the case, as argued by Renaissance theorists (after Aristotle), then the play would lack **unity**. Or could two plots, though of equal importance, be related to the same action, thus having a split focus? (See **perspective**; **episode**.)

DOWN STAGE

That portion of the stage closest to the audience, so named from the Renaissance/Baroque stages which were raked up from front to back to accomodate **perspective** set designs. Movements downstage are the most powerful. (See **upstage.**)

DRAMA

(Greek: "deed; to do") In common usage, the word (like the word "play") has been used for both the script and the event. In an effort to mitigate possible confusion (or to facilitate dramaturgical precision), "drama" has come to refer exclusively to the play text in its written mode, that is, as *potential* **theatre**.

Drama then can be defined as: the present imitation of human relationships in crisis. In this definition:

"present" means that the **action** is conducted in the here and now, not in the narrative past; in the form of **dialogue**, not description;

"imitation" reminds us that drama is a representation, not reality, and is thus a *constructed* **artifact**, which has a significant, but imaginative connection to reality;

"human relationships" are the fundamental subjects of drama. Since the primary human relationship is two (see **duet**), at any given moment in a play a binary relationship is the focus of the **action**-- even a monologue involves an internal debate (e.g., "to be or not to be") and a **direct address** is in practice a binary discourse (the audience treated as "community"). (Important binary relationships also exist between a character and a prop, "is this a dagger I see before me?" or between a character and the setting, "so foul and fair a day I have not seen." Samuel Beckett's *Krapp's Last Tape,* a single character play, explores and stretches the dramaturgical limits of the binary relationship: Krapp talks to himself, to props ("spooooool"), to the audience and to recorded selves at earlier ages;

"in crisis" refers to the demonstrable fact that human relationships are inherently unstable. In drama this is reflected in **issues** *between characters*--which evolve through time to major and minor crises which in turn result in changing situations. To say, therefore, that "drama means conflict" is to trivialize a complex, dynamic *process.*

DRAMATIC CRITICISM

The analysis and critique of dramatic texts and their representation on the stage. Historically, dramatic criticism begins with Aristotle (*Poetics*, ca. 335 B.C.), Horace (*The Art of Poetry*, ca. 24 B.C.) and Longinus (*On the Sublime*, ca. 100 A.D.) and it re-emerged in the Italian Renaissance with the humanists (e.g., Lodovico Castelvetro, *On Aristotle's Poetics*, 1570). Since that time dramatic criticism has taken many forms (subsumed under the term **dramaturgy**) and has been presented from a number of different perspectives--influenced by time and place--but essentially it has focused on a limited number of problems:

1. Structure (**plot**): the issue of causality vs. chance, etc.;
2. Character & behaviour: e.g., **decorum** vs. environment and heredity;

3. Genre: purity of form vs. hybridization;

4. Style: "realism," "expressionism," "Epic," etc.;

5. Conventions (of text, performance, production);

6. Multi-modal presentation;

7. Acting, and theories of;

8. Directing and textual interpretation;

9. Reception;

10. Social function.

Recently, feminist dramatic criticism has re-examined both drama and theatre (and thus dramatic criticism) from the perspective of **gender** bias (see, e.g., Adrienne Rich, "When we Dead Awaken: Writing as Revision").[25]

DRAMATIC IRONY

An incongruity between the knowledge possessed by one branch of the **performance triad** and at least one of the others. Usually, dramatic irony refers to the audience's superior knowledge vis a vis an individual or group on stage, but theoretically, any individual or group can possess greater knowledge than all the rest, thus gaining an ironic perspective.

In **comedy** the audience and the hero are often allied in terms of knowledge, and this can be one of the reasons for audience empathy. In **farce** it is often the wiley servant who has superior knowledge (see **trickster**), while in **tragedy** it is the hero who is ignorant and left in the dark until the end. The detective hero is defined as one who acquires knowledge ahead of everyone else (except the villain) and acts on it.

Dramaturgically, we should focus on the playwright's control of information: who knows what and who is left out. Once the playwright has established a situation involving such an incongruity, he can then control the moment when the ignorant group and/or individual learns the full truth. (See **recognition, scene a faire;**

---

[25]From *Lies, Secrets and Silence: Selected Prose,* 1966-1978, 1979.

theatrical irony; exposition.)

DRAMATIC STRUCTURE

(See **plot**)

DRAMATURGE

With this French spelling and from its Greek origins, the word simply means "playwright," but the German *dramaturg* refers to another function--allied to, but distinct from playwriting. The dramaturg has traditionally functioned as a textual advisor to a theatre company. This could be anything from translation to an analysis of the **dramaturgy** of the text; from bringing scholarship to bear on the historical and cultural aspects of a text to advice on the company's repertoire; from formal (in house) critiques to archives and publicity; from assistance to the director, designer and cast to assistance to a playwright with a new script. The latter role has been predominant in North American theatre where the director has reigned supreme.

The first (formal) dramaturg in Germany was G.E. Lessing (1729-81), playwright and theorist and advisor to the Hamburg Theatre. His *Hamburgische Dramaturgie* (1768) is a collection of his critical writing on the emerging German national theatre.[26] In England, the most famous "literary advisor" was Kenneth Tynan, appointed by Laurence Olivier to the National Theatre in 1963. In the United States and Canada, resistance to the employment of dramaturgs has waned over the past 20 years, with many companies using dramaturgs in the development of new plays and repertoire.

The dramaturg is therefore (ideally) a theatrical and cultural generalist, a resource person and a critic.

---

[26]For modern dramaturgical theory see Manfred Pfister, *The Theory and Analysis of Drama*, trans. by John Halliday (New York: Cambridge Univ. Press, 1988, 1977).

DRAMATURGY

(Greek: "dramatic composition") Webster's Dictionary defines dramaturgy as "the art and technique of dramatic writing and theatrical representation."[27] This is useful in the distinction made between text and performance and in the dictionary's recognition of the craft and art involved in both; but "art" and "technique" are too vague to be helpful. To this definition it is therefore useful to add the notion of *creating* and/or *interpreting* **code systems** and **conventions** which will affect the sounds, images and movements of performance.

The study and practice of dramaturgy, then, can be described in terms of four interlocking branches:

1. TEXTUAL DRAMATURGY: refers to the *embedded codes and conventions* which are unique to dramatic composition and which serve as guides to theatrical representation. These codes are embedded by the playwright into the dialogue itself. Such codes include, for example, deictic references, **given circumstances**, entrances and exits, characters, references to **offstage life** and so on. Textual analysis, in practice, is a matter of exposing these codes in order to create a **performance text**.

2. PERFORMANCE DRAMATURGY: refers to the *interpretive* code systems of the **mise en scene**, or the staged representation of a text. These codes utilize three fundamental communication channels: aural, visual and kinetic (all of the sights, sounds and movements of performance).

3. PRODUCTION DRAMATURGY: refers to elements of theatrical production: theatre architecture, stage/auditorium relationships, stage and lighting equipment, seating systems and similar considerations-- all of which are also communicative code systems affecting performance and reception.

4. RECEPTION DRAMATURGY: refers to a spectator's *decoding* of the code systems presented during performance. Thus, the demographics of audience composition are particularly relevant: age,

---

[27]*Webster's Ninth New Collegiate Dictionary,* Frederick C. Mish, ed. (Springfield: Merriam-Webster, 1983), p. 381.

gender, education, occupation and class.   Ultimately, reception dramaturgy is the location of *meaning* and is consequently relative to individual understanding.

Because any dramatic text or theatrical performance is an expression of and influence on the culture of which it is a part, **social function** becomes an integral part of dramaturgical analysis. This involves consideration of the ideological assumptions of the time, the power structures of the society, the purpose art is intended to serve for those who patronize it, fluctuations in taste and in the value given to art, and the changing relation of the artist to society.

(See E. Ashton and G. Savona, *Theatre as Sign System: a Semiotics of Text and Performance*, 1991; Susan Bennett, *Theatre Audiences: a Theory of Production and Reception*, 1990 ; Kier Elam, *The Semiotics of Theatre and Drama*, 1980.)

DRAME

Middle class drama; a genre theoretically treating the problems of the middle class in a serious way, as distinct from **bourgeois tragedy** which produced moral lessons for the middle class--object lessons on the consequences of "immoral" behaviour. Denis Diderot (1713-84) in France, along with G.E. Lessing (1729-81) in Germany are credited with developing the form and its theoretical basis. Drame should also be compared to the following century's **thesis play**. The three forms were ancestral to the plays of Ibsen and his contemporaries and to modern drama in general.

(See Diderot's prefaces to *The Illigitimate Son*, 1757; *The Paterfamilias*, 1758; see also Lessing's *Hamburg Dramaturgy*, 1757; *Miss Sara Sampson* , 1755.)

DUET

A scene involving two characters; the binary basis of all **drama**, that is, the prime *relationship*. A scene with just two characters has qualities not found in any other combination, such as a sense of privacy (conspiracy, love etc.): the two characters can speak freely and directly (if they wish) without the constraints of an audience (see **trio**).

If an entire play has just two characters, certain simple, but significant dramaturgical consequences follow. Primary among these is the possible number and composition of **french scenes**:

> 1. brief periods with an empty stage are possible (with the potential of an active **offstage life**);

> 2. either character A or B can appear alone on stage as solos;

> 3. or characters A and B can appear as a duet;

> 4. while these possibilities are all the playwright has to work with in a two character play, they can be used in any order, for any length of time and as often as desired.

Playwrights have often explored and stretched the limits of the two-handed play with interesting effects. Harold Pinter's *The Dumb Waiter*, for example, is a two character play with the addition of a very active mechanical prop. The dumb waiter, which makes occasional and unexpected appearances, functions as a bizarre third character with "lines" in the form of enigmatic messages. Similarly, the addition of a telephone can add the effect of a third character on the action. Samuel Beckett's *Happy Days* is a two character play with one partner silent, nearly immobile and practically out of sight.

Two character scenes in a play with a larger cast provide opportunities for more intense one-on-one confrontations, conspiracies or love scenes; a series of duets involving different combinations of characters allows the playwright to demonstrate **character** evolving in different situations.

DUMB SHOW

A term referring to a Renaissance practice of showing a summary of the action in mime as prologue to the play as a whole, to an Act, or even to a scene, as in the dumb show which precedes Hamlet's "Mousetrap" (see **Senecan**). The practice no doubt was necessitated by the conditions of the commercial performance as both an attention grabber and an aid to following a complex plot, especially for the uneducated. Dramaturgically, the device could be used to place the action of the play, Act or scene in perspective: the audience would know beforehand how the action would unfold, thus placing attention on character and motivation.

E

EIRON

(Greek: "dissembler") One of the three main roles in ancient comedy identified in the Roman *Tractatus Coislinianus* (see *alazon, bomolochus*). The *eiron* is one who says less than he knows and one who functions as a deflator of pretension (see also **trickster**).

EKKYKLEMA

(Greek: "cart; wagon") (See **stage machinery**.)

EMBEDDED

Code systems are "organic" when they appear within the actual dialogue of the text. Embedded codes cannot be ignored by directors and actors, whereas **scene directions** often are. For example, when a character says, "close the curtains and come over here and sit beside me on the couch," these furnishings must be present and movement must occur (unless in the next line the other character refuses).

EMOTIONAL MEMORY

"Affective memory" or "emotional recall:" these are terms used by Stanislavski and his followers to describe a method of stimulating emotion in performance.[28] Later repudiated by Stanislavski, the process involved a deliberate effort of an actor to recall the emotions felt in an actual, personal life experience which was at least analogous to the present dramatic situation and *reliving* this experience in the context of character and performance.

The process caused controversy because it tended to have a counter-productive effect on the actor (or acting student), that is, a focus on the self at the expense of the character and situation.

EMPATHY

In the theatre, empathy denotes emotional identification with a character (or performer) on stage, whereas *sympathy* refers more to a positive understanding. Empathy, along with vicarious and autonomic responses to physical action on stage, are generally in conflict with **aesthetic distance**--to an indeterminate degree, identification increases at the expense of objectivity.

ENVIRONMENTAL THEATRE

As distinct from "environments," which are visual art creations, environmental theatre is a form of **happening** in which the environmental experiences of the participants (audiences) are foregrounded. Environmental theatre refers to the dramaturgy of the audience/performance/space relationship and to the many forms this can take in various types of performance, from circus to street theatre to side shows to the proscenium stage.

(See Richard Scheckner, *Dionysus in 69, By Means of Performance* and "Six Axioms for Environmental Theatre," in *Public Domain*, 1969.)

EPIC THEATRE

(See **figure 6: "Theatre Relationships"**) The dramaturgical style of

---

[28]Constantin Stanislavsky, *An Actor Prepares,* trans. by Elizabeth Reynolds Hapgood (New York: Theatre Arts Books, 1936), chapter 9, "Emotion Memory."

"Brechtian" or "non-Aristotelian" theatre. The term stands for a combination of **conventions** and techniques developed by Bertolt Brecht and Erwin Piscator in Germany between the wars. Together, these techniques are intended to place the events of the performance in a radically different perspective than that created by the traditional theatre of illusion. Foremost among these are:

> 1. historisation: placing events in the past, or selecting subjects from the past in order to break from the aesthetics of the "here and now;"
>
> 2. scale: large ("epic") scale production as compared to intimate theatre;
>
> 3. mixtures of the narrative and dramatic modes (i.e., strong elements of story telling as a framework for dramatic action);
>
> 4. mixtures of speech and song to break dramatic continuity;
>
> 5. a freedom to move the action through time and space in a non-sequential structure (thus breaking the **"unities"**).

Epic theatre under Brecht also came to be associated with other aspects of his dramaturgical theories, including:

> 1. *"verfremdungseffekt"* (German: "to make strange"): aesthetic and social objectivity; "alienation" or "estrangement;" increasing **aesthetic distance** between the audience, characters and situation;
>
> 2. **mixed media:** the use of film, slides, recorded sound, posters etc. as complementary **code systems** in order to break the continuity of illusion created by live presence; with Brecht, however, these systems functioned as competing, not complementary, media again to maximize aesthetic distance; similarly, production elements such as lighting instruments, flies and scene shifting were exposed to foreground the essential *theatricality* of the play;
>
> 3. *"gestus"* (German: "gesture"): characters are conceived and played in terms of their social circumstances and attitudes, not personal objectives. This implies a shift away from a focus on characters' inner lives to an analysis of their social behaviour to each other. Each scene is written and performed as a basic *"grundgestus"* or political idea ("grand gesture"). In other words, *gestus* refers to a symbolic

gesture or tableau which crystallizes the social essence of the scene: e.g., when, in a courtroom, all rise on the entrance of the judge, they rise in deference to authority, tradition and even ideology. In epic theatre such a moment is foregrounded as a *gestus*.

(See Elizabeth Wright, *Postmodern Brecht*, 1989; John Willett, *The Theatre of Erwin Piscator*, 1979; Erwin Piscator, *The Political Theatre, a History*, 1978; John Willet, trans, *Brecht on Theatre*, 1964.)

EPILOGUE

(Greek: *epilogos*, "afterword") A concluding scene or speech, often witten in verse, was usually spoken by the leading actor (in Restoration and 18th century productions). It is not known how often the epilogue was used in Greek theatre (so few plays have survived), but the implication exists that the epilogue was part of the formal structure of performance (see **exodos**). Epilogues were often used in **baroque** theatre as formal appeals or "apologies;" they are only used occasionally in modern times (e.g., in **epic theatre**).

EPISODE

(Greek: *epeisodios,* "coming in besides") A self contained scene of some duration (see also **french scene**); a section of the **plot** dealing with a specific **issue** or **incident**; the formal divisions of a Greek **tragedy** (episodes alternate with **stasima**).

In derogatory terms, an "episodic" play is one whose scenes are not all organically linked to a central **action**, resulting in a play which lacks unity. Historically, the medieval tradition supported episodic structures (hence the mystery cycles and the Elizabethan "**double plot**), while the "rules" of **neoclassicism** attempted to counter such practices (see **unities**).

EURYTHMICS

"Invented" by Jacques Dalcroze (1865-1960), Eurythmics taught that *rhythm* is the basis of all art and that the performer must respond first of all to the basic rhythms of a work or situation or suggestion. His classes tended to focus on dance as a physical response to the rhythm of music, not to melody or structure or abstract (programatic) idea. His work and ideas were an important influence on the scenic theories of Adolphe Appia, who sought the rhythm embedded in the text of a play as the basis of scene design.

(See Appia's *Music and Stage Setting*, 1899; *The Work of Living Art*, 1921.)

EXODOS

(Greek: "the way out") A choral ode performed by the chorus of a Greek tragedy (or comedy) as it left the stage. Its structural function was minimal, but its purpose was to leave the audience with a final thought or summation or "moral." Dramaturgically, the entrance and exit of the chorus were fundamental codes suggesting that the "public" significance of the action was about to begin or end (see **chorus**).

EXPOSITION

Essential information about characters' past lives and relationships, the circumstances and incidents revealled by the playwright near the beginning of a play as introductory detail, or throughout the play as a structural device. Those plays which begin *in media res* and whose actions depend on the past, rely heavily on expository techniques. Thus the tradition which begins with Sophocles' *Oedipus* (with its technique of a gradually revealed past and a growing awareness of the *consequences* of that past), ends (effectively) with Ibsen (e.g., *Hedda Gabler, Ghosts*). This is to say that the dramaturgical *technique* of expository writing has not effectively progressed beyond that point, although it is still being used. (See also **given circumstances**.)

EXPRESSIONISM

(See **figure 5: "expressionism"**) An **avant garde**, post WWI movement in the arts; a "sub stream" of **romanticism**, influenced in part by a growing interest in the psychology of the unconscious and in part by a growing disillusionment with the power structures and values, artistic sterility and/or "scientism" of western culture (see **realism, naturalism**).

In the visual arts, the movement was led by pre war painters like Edvard Munsch (*The Scream*, 1885), who also created stage designs for Strindberg and Ibsen, Oskar Kokaschka *The Tragedy of Man*, 1908, and Marc Chagall, *Self Portrait with Seven Fingers*, 1911. Expressionism in music is illustrated by some of the works of Bartok, Berg, Hindemith and Schonberg. Extreme contrasts in pitch, dissonance, instrumentation, dynamics and rhythm are interpreted as direct expressions of extreme emotional states.

Expressionism in the theatre was concerned with breaking through the superficial, empirical style of **realism** and the impersonal sociology of **naturalism**. Expressionist playwrights such as Franz Wedekind (*Spring's Awakening*, 1891), August Strindberg *(The Dream Play*, 1902), and Ernst Toller (*Masses and Man*, 1921) led the way with experiments in dramatic structure, autobiographical material, performance style and scene design. Expressionists, whether obsessed with style or political issues, typically produced works of a highly subjective, if not completely autobiographical nature. The resulting images, sounds and movements appearing on stage were thus *distorted* by their passage through a psyche *in extremis*. They were intended to be projections of the artist's tortured alienation, anxiety, frustrations, guilt and phobias--in other words, concrete manifestations of nightmares.

(See Sigmund Freud, *The Interpretation of Dreams*, 1900; Walter H. Sokel, *The Writer in Extremis*, 1959; John Willett, *Expressionism*; 1970 Lionel Richard, *The Phaidon Encyclopedia of Expressionism*, 1978.)

EXTRAVAGANZA

An elaborate form of **music theatre** in the early development of **musical**

comedy in America; a light music hall entertainment in 19th century England. The extravaganza, like the follies, which emphasized spectacular costumes and scenery and chorus lines, had little or no story, but relied on sheer spectacle and popular music (see **revue, vaudeville**). The form was interpreted in early film musicals by Busby Birkeley.

F

FABLE

As applied to **drama**, the fable is the story line or **plot** of a play. In Latin, however, the word is used in conjunction with several forms of ancient drama as a prefix, e.g., *"fabula Atellana,"* or Atellan farce.

FALLING ACTION

(See **denouement, resolution;** see also **Freytag's pyramid**.)

FARCE

(See **figure 1: "The Ur Drama, Winter"**) Renaissance, Baroque and Victorian theorists have generally included farce as one of the various forms of **comedy**--usually as a lower, more physical and bawdy type. The opinion has more or less continued into the 20th century. On closer examination, however, it appears that the reasons for maintaining this low opinion of the genre were more ideological than aesthetic or dramaturgical. It is certainly true that there is a comic hierarchy ranging from the sedate and witty through the rough and tumble of slapstick and that all of these forms involve humour. Nevertheless, since Aristotle argued that comedy was concerned with the activities of "worse than average" people,[29] it seemed to follow that farce was simply concerned with the very lowest or most common taste (in the audience) and the worst sort of behaviour (among characters).

---

[29]Aristotle, *Poetics,* chap. 5, 1449a, 1-10.

Comedy presents us with the imperfections of human nature; farce entertains us with what is monstrous and chimerical. The one causes laughter in those who can judge of men and manners; the other produces the same effect in those who can do neither.[30]

Farce confronts both characters and audience with threats of *anarchy*: physical, social, sexual, mental and/or linguistic. Farce is aggressive, relentless and merciless in its exposure of pretension and abnormality. Farce employs violence, trickery and subversion; amorality, mockery and the wildest of coincidence in its pursuit of these ends. As a consequence, farce can present the outlines or premonition of a very demonic world, and it is no wonder that an elite class would abhor such a prospect or avoid such "entertainment."

The dramaturgical ancestor of farce was not Aristophanic comedy, but the Greek **satyr play**, which was a licentious, irreverent parody of tragedy, legend, epic or myth. The spirit of farce is represented by a **trickster** figure (see Carl Jung: *Four Archetypes: Mother, Rebirth, Spirit, Trickster*, 1959; see also **vice, fool**). A prototype is Silenus, tutor of Dionysus, and character in (at least) Sophocles' *Cyclops*.

All of this is not to say that the elements of the farcical do not appear in comedy. Such figures and scenes often appear as mechanisms to further the ends of the comic hero and heroine in their quest to defeat the old order. It is in this sense that servants in comedy, as members of the lowest social order, serve both the hero and heroine as the spirit of farce. Sometimes these farcical elements predominate in a play (e.g., in Roman comedy, in **commedia dell'Arte**), while the celebratory **action** of the play and its hero and the renewal of society through their union becomes distinctly secondary. Pure farces are thus relatively rare.

It should finally be noted that the target of farce is often dramatic convention itself. Structural unity is destroyed by coincidence and pure chance, characters are not always as they appear and **decorum** is often not observed. See *Pierre Pathelin*

---

[30]John Dryden, "Preface to an Evening's Love," in Dukore, *Dramatic Theory and Criticism*, p. 334.

as an example of medieval farce, and Feydeau's *A Flea in Her Ear*, as an example of 19th century farce. "Monty Python's Flying Circus" and "Fawlty Towers" are pure examples of television farce.

(See also Eric Bentley, "Farce," in *The Life of the Drama*, 1964 and J.M. Davis, *Farce*, 1978.)

FEEDBACK LOOP

(From cybernetics, or communication and control theory) The internal structure of a **french scene** is composed of feedback loops, or conversational initiative / response / adjustment units (**beats**) conducted by the characters in the scene. Each character pursues a private agenda (see **objective**) with **tactics** aimed at maximizing personal success. The limits of a beat are thus defined by the initiator of a feedback loop: when an initiative is made, a new beat begins.

Feedback loops mark the details of the playwright's control over the lives of his characters. Deep analysis, of particular interest to both actors and directors, must therefore focus on the feedback structure of beats: who initiates and why, the nature of the response, the types of adjustment necessary to maintain one's objective, when and how the beat is terminated (by whom and for what reason) and who initiates the next beat.

Consider the following exchange in which "A" is an abusive father and "B" is his daughter:

> **A: Sing for me.**
> **B: I can't.**
> **A: You can.**
> **B: I can't sing.**
> **A: You can.**

The words here might be simple and repetitive, but driven by tactical intentions within a specific situation (neither is indicated organically in the fragment), they can communicate an on-going relationship of surprising depth. To illustrate:

> **A** initiates with a demand (or request);
> **B** responds negatively with a vague excuse;

> A decides to adjust his tactics, while keeping the same objective (to
>   get **A** to sing; to exercise control over **A**);
> **B** adjusts in turn with a clarification (or excuse: "I can't sing");
> **A** counters this by denying the validity of **B**'s reason.

With this last line there is an implied finality (if not threat), as though the beat is being terminated and we expect a new beat to begin. But **B** might continue to resist, raising the tension ever higher until the beat is terminated by **A** or **B** (thus a **climax**) or by an interruption, such as the entrance of another character.

(See Robert Cohen, *Acting Power*, 1978.)

FESTIVE THEATRE

(See **figure 12**) Displaced festivals of renewal--musical comedy, in particular-- celebrate the regeneration of the community through the synergy of the **multi-modal communication system**. The combination of drama, music, dance, scenery and virtuoso performance are the collective means, the hero and heroine (and their helpers) are the agents, and communal renewal is the objective. Festive theatre and festivals of renewal have four structural components:

1. **Display:** some means by which the community (on stage or off) can review, proclaim or celebrate its important values, traditions and accomplishments. In festivals of renewal display can take many forms, such as parades, craft shows and special projects; on stage, the performance of scenes in a succession of locations constitutes a display for the larger community represented by the audience. In *Oklahoma!*, by Rodgers and Hammerstein (1943), for example, scenes of prairie skies and corn fields, farm yards, the "smokehouse" and the "box social" are **icons** of the American West.

2. **Contest:** festivals of renewal typically highlight a formal ritual combat which usually symbolizes a culture specific event and value system or tradition, while at the same time recalling more archetypal events, such as the defeat of evil or darkness, or the passing of the old year and the coming of the new. The conflict between the genera-tions (or some variation) in musical comedy is simply a **displacement** of such ritual contests. In *Oklahoma!* the forces of darkness are personified by Jud Fry, and his death clears the way for celebration.

3. **Celebration:** in festivals of renewal, the victory of the forces of regeneration is celebrated with banquets, dancing and similar activities; in musical comedy the victory of the hero and heroine over the forces of the old society (often parent figures) or of evil is celebrated with a wedding and the anticipation of a fertile union. The "shivaree" in *Oklahoma!* is part of this celebration and anticipation. One aspect of the "festive style" of musical comedy is that the audience is implicity included in the celebrations: major song and dance numbers are "turned out" and the audience responds with applause; the final curtain call acknowledges the importance of the audience to the new order, and the audience in turn joins the festivity with applause.

4. **Ceremony:** festivals of renewal are not everyday events. Some formal recognition of this fact and the special importance of the festival in the life of the community is made through speeches, opening and closing ceremonies, awards and entertainment. In musical comedy, the formal seating, the dimmed lights, the tuning of the orchestra and the arrival of the conductor, the overture (itself a displacement of the courtly fanfare), the rising of the curtain and stage lights and the final curtain call all constitute a displaced ceremonial recognition that this is a special event. Within *Oklahoma!* the mock trial of Curly, the weddings and the reprise of "Oh What a Beautiful Mornin'," together with the full cast curtain call serve as a ritual of closure.

Considered from this perspective, both festivals of renewal and musical comedies (through **displacement**) are "rites of passage:" in the first instance the passage of the individual to adulthood through testing and community celebration; in the second case, it is the community which passes from one existential state to another through the struggles of the hero and heroine. Both Curly and Laurie must pass tests of maturity, while Oklahoma must pass through its "adolescence" as a feuding Territory to become a State and a full member of the Union.

As the ultimate **MMCS** in theatre, the musical achieves its transcendant objective through the **synergy** of speech, song, music, dance and scenery. *Oklahoma!* was a milestone in the development of American musical comedy for this very reason: for the first time on the American stage all modes of communication were *organically* integrated through plot, character and action.

In terms of **social function**, communal transcendence is supported by a celebration of current ideology. In the case of *Oklahoma!*, written just after Pearl Harbour and performed for wartime America, the celebration of statehood and the civilizing principles of the American middle class were met with overwhelming audience approval.

(See Arnold van Gennep, *The Rites of Passage*, 1969; Mircea Eliade, *The Myth of the Eternal Return*, 1954; Carl Jung, *Four Archetypes: Mother, Rebirth, Spirit, Trickster*, 1959; R. Kerry White, *Historic Festivals and the Nature of Musical Comedy*, 1984.)

FIGURA (FIGURE, TYPE, TYPOLOGY)

(Latin: figure) In medieval cosmology, historical events, people, animals and things accounted in the Old Testament prefigure or anticipate parallels in the New Testament. In this sense, the Bible is a description of the divine plan to redeem mankind. Thus a lamb is a *type* of Christ, the Temptation of Adam *prefigures* the Temptation of Christ, etc.

This notion has specific and important relevance to medieval theatre and drama, especially to the **mystery cycles**, which are dramatizations of such a view of history. The dramaturgical structure of a mystery cycle, then, is not simply a matter of chronology, it is a matter of prediction and fulfillment.

(See Erich Auerbach, "Figura," in *Scenes from the Drama of European Literature*, 1959.)

FLUXUS

An **avant garde** descendant of the **dada** movement, Fluxus, along with **Happenings** were among the the anti-academic, anti traditional art movements of the 1960's. The first Fluxus event, Nam June Paik's *Neo-Dada in der Musik*, Dusseldorf,

1962, and various "Fluxus festivals" set this variant apart from Happenings.[31] Fluxus events were those anyone could perform, events devoid of symbolism and expression on the part of the performer, events employing chance and events which "ridiculed academic art and cultural traditions and having a pleasant time whilst doing so."[32]

FOCAL CHARACTER

Technically and historically a term from the study of optics, the *focal point* and thus the focal character come from the Italian Renaissance and the development of single point **perspective** (see **figure 11** and **POV**). In both cases, the reference is not to a dramatic character, but to the "Godly Prince" seated in the auditorium. The scene on stage is conceived *as though projected from his eye*, while he himself is as much the focus of attention as any character on stage. It is in this sense that both *focal point* and *POV* have been used in the motion picture industry.

In **expressionist drama,** with its highly subjective point of view, the term came to refer to the central character (**protagonist**) whose experience governs the action.

FOIL

In *King Lear*, the loyal Duke of Kent is banished by the King in the first scene. He then "goes underground" by adopting a disguise in order to continue to serve his king. In the play as a whole, Kent has approximately 11% of the total lines, whereas Lear has 24%; however, Kent is on stage for approximately 54% of the play's time--as much or more than any other character, including Lear. This is not simply a case of being seen and not heard, but of Kent's **dramatic function**: he is intended to serve as a *foil* to the extremes of evil and madness in the kingdom, a

---

[31]Tomas Schmit, "A Fluxus Farewell to Perfection," an interview by Gunter Berghaus in *The Drama Review*, T141, Spring, 1944, pp. 79-97.

[32]ibid., p. 82.

"touchstone" of the Good.

FOLIO

(From Latin: "leaf") Any loose sheet(s) of paper or case for carrying loose sheets (such as sketches), the term in drama comes from the printing practices of Elizabethan and Jacobean London where a folio was a full sheet of printing paper. It was usually folded into two parts for convenience and used for the complete works of an author (e.g., the first "folio" of Shakespeare). The folio was also divided into four parts (**quarto**) for the printing of individual works. The scholarly efforts of nearly 400 years have been devoted to determining the "best" versions of Shakespeare's plays from the folios and quartos printed at the time as well as after his death.

From a dramaturgical point of view, these practices and scholarly efforts illustrate the changing value attached to the dramatic text. In Shakespeare's time (and before), the text as a published work was a distinctly secondary consideration. Of considerably more importance was the performance of the text, which changed with rehearsal and subsequent performances. After Shakespeare's time, the dramatic text became valued as *literature*--so much so that its primarily function as a "blueprint" for performance tended to be forgotten. In the modern theatre, this original purpose and value of the script has reappeared.

FOOL

An interesting (and somewhat mysterious) recurrent character in Elizabethan and Jacobean drama, the Fool has several possible antecedents with cross-cultural parallels. In Renaissance courts the Fool or court jester was a licensed clown, hired to entertain. In the drama he could function as a **foil** as well as a clown / musician / satirist. In *King Lear* the Fool's activities are particularly poignant as he attempts to keep the King on an even keel. He disappears from the play in Act III once the crisis of madness and storm have passed.

Antecedents include the **Vice** figure from medieval morality plays, the **Feast of Fools**, and the professional **clown**. However, the Fool is also a variant of the trickly slave from Roman comedy (see *eiron, bomolochus*) and as such the archetype of all comic servants, even the **sidekick** of the Hollywood cowboy.

(See C. Jung, *Four Archetypes: Trickster*, 1959; Enid Welsford, *The Fool*, 1968; see also **farce**.)

FORESHADOWING

A structural technique to prepare the audience for an event later in the play, thus creating anticipation and suspense.

FOURTH WALL

A **convention** which dictates that the audience and stage are separated by an invisible "fourth wall." The purpose of this convention is to foster illusionism, that is, the acceptance that what is happening on stage is both a "real, but a separate actuality. The fourth wall convention is thus most suited to **representational** styles such as **realism**. To "break the fourth wall" is to acknowledge the presence of the audience. The fourth wall convention was instrumental in the development of **sub text** as it made **asides** and **soliloquies** unacceptable.

FREEZE

A **convention** of **performance dramaturgy** whereby an actor will stop in mid motion, while action continues around him--presumably in a separate space / time continuum. The "frozen" character(s), by convention, cannot be see by others, although he may be pretending, and thus himself be able to see and hear.

FRENCH SCENE

A term derived from the editors of French texts who began a new scene with the entrance and/or exit of characters, the "french scene" is defined as a period of time on stage in which the number of characters remains the same--*regardless of length* (but see **systemic change**). The french scene is the fundamental structural mechanism under the playwright's control, and is thus a basic unit of dramaturgical analysis. The playwright controls, in other words, how many characters will be on stage from moment to moment and thus who can speak to or interact with whom at every point in the play (see **figures 8 (A & B): "Graphic Displays"**).

The addition or deletion of a character to or from the stage profoundly affects audience perception and thus "meaning:" even the entrance and brief **presence** of a silent maid can interrupt or change the direction of the conversation on stage. What had been a private **duet**, for example, momentarily becomes a public **trio**.

The french scenes in a play consequently control its fundamental **rhythm**: the coming and going of characters and the changing composition of characters on stage for various lengths of time are the primary building blocks of dramatic structure.

FREYTAG'S PYRAMID

Gustav Freytag's *Techniques of Drama* (1863)[33] is a basic work of textual **dramaturgy** which summarizes the rhetorical theories of drama since the Renaissance. It has since been superseded by much more empirical and flexible notions of dramatic structure. In this work, Freytag attempts to make the case that drama, because it is conflict based, follows a strict pattern (shaped like a pyramid), from **inciting moment** and **exposition** through **rising action** or **complication** to a **climax** and back down through a **falling action** to a **catastrophe** and finally a **resolution** or **denouement**.

(See Volker Klotz, *Open and closed Forms in Drama*, 1960; Manfred Pfister, *The Theory and Analysis of Drama*, 1977.)

---

[33]Gustav Freytag, *Techniques of Drama: an Exposition of Dramatic Composition and Art*, trans. by E.J. MacEwen (New York: Scribners, 1968).

FRINGE THEATRE

See **alternative theatre**

FUTURISM

A movement of the early Italian **avant garde** led by F.T. Marinetti (1876-1944) which espoused a political-aesthetic doctrine in favour of modern technology and against all of the encumbrances of the past. The movement and its followers became associated with the Italian proto-fascists and glorified war as a culture's most vital expression of machine, energy and vitality.

Marinetti's *The founding Manifesto of Futurism* (1909) was just one of a series of proclamations and manifestos of the movement--it was a characteristic of the avant garde to proclaim revolutionary principles. After the war, the futurist movement produced plays and other "events," but leadership soon passed to the visual artist, Enrico Prampolini (1894-1960), whose abstract, mechanistic stage designs and advocacy of marionettes influenced several other movements and artists, from **constructivism** to **happenings** and from Meyerhold to Craig.

(See Michael Kirby, *Futurist Performance*, 1971.)

G

GALLERY

Another name for balcony seating in theatres ranging from the Elizabethan Globe to the 19th century Drury Lane. Galleries generally denote class-structured seating, but not always of the same value from theatre to theatre. Seats in the Globe's galleries were more expensive than standing in the **pit**, whereas gallery seats in late 19th century commercial theatres and opera houses were cheaper than seats in either the orchestra or boxes.

GALLOWS HUMOUR

Morbid humour concerned with death, torture or disfigurement. The range of such humour includes medieval plays with **Vice** figures and despots (such as Herod), Renaissance plays which find grizzly humour in death and torture (like the "gravediggers' scene" in *Hamlet*), the dastardly deeds of villains in 19th century melodramas and the two-sided barbs in modern tragicomedies, from Chekhov's *The Seagull* to Beckett's *Waiting for Godot*.

GENDER

Western drama and theatre have traditionally supported a gender bias: most published and performed plays were written by men, from a male perspective in patriarchal societies; most plays implicitly supported the perpetuation of this bias; most societies (until the 17th century) did not allow women on the stage (many frowned on women in the audience); most plays as a consequence had relatively few female roles of any significance; most critical theory and dramaturgical analysis was conducted by men. (There have been exceptions to these rules, but they are rare: the Empress Theodora (6th century AD), who married Justinian, Emperor of the Eastern Roman Empire, was an actress (which means she was not the only one); Hrosvitha of Gandersheim, a Bendedictine Abbess in the 10th century, was an important playwright; Catherine and Maria de Medici, Henrietta of Denmark (Queen to Charles I) were powerful producers of *ballets* and **masques**--and performed in them).

Lately, however, the balance has begun to shift. Far more women are writing plays which are produced, especially in North America; there are far more good roles for women; many women have become directors and there is now a substantial body of feminist dramaturgical theory and criticism. The result of this shift has been a growing awarness of all concerned in the theatre, not just of the nature of this new perspective, but also of the "relativism" of all such perspectives applied to the creation, interpretation and reception of art.

(See Sue Ellen Case, *Feminism and Theatre*, 1986 and editor, *Performing Feminism: Feminist Critical Theory and Theatre*, 1990; Gayle Austin, *Feminist Theories for Criticism*, 1990.)

GENRE

(See **figure 1: "The Ur Drama"**) Grouping works of art according to shared characteristics in both form and content has had a long and varied history. From Aristotle until recently, all drama was listed as a literary genre, along with epic, lyric and novel because they all had a basis in language. Now, drama, literature, film, dance, music, painting etc. are seen as *modes of communication*, each having generic sub categories (hence the differences also between **dramaturgy**, **rhetoric**, poetics, art and music theory as branches of aesthetics). *How* a work communicates and affects its audience is as important as *what* is being communicated. The various sub genres of drama--**tragedy, comedy, melodrama, farce, tragicomedy** and their various offshoots, such as **sentimental comedy, bourgeois tragedy, festive theatre-** -are thus sub modes of communication. A tragedy communicates differently with its audience than a comedy: it has a different means, different types of characters and a different tone--all in order to produce different effects.

A polarity, suggested by Aristotle, is implied between the "principle" genres (tragedy and comedy): tragedy deals with leaders in a lofty, serious style, while comedy deals with lower classes in a familiar, humorous style.[34] Tragedy impresses us emotionally with the greatness of its characters; comedy makes us laugh by ridiculing the behaviour of those "less than us." This polarity is founded on notions of social class as seen from an elitist point of view. On the other hand, Aristotle can be forgiven if his empirical survey turned up nothing but tragedies about aristocrats and comedies about common people.

One of the most comprehensive theories of genres is that proposed by Northrop Frye in which genre is related to a natural or "archetypal" life cycle, with **comedy** being associated with spring, **melodrama** and romance with summer, **tragedy** with fall and both **tragicomedy and farce** (or irony and satire) with winter. Each natural phase can then be sub divided according to the work's proximity to one of the natural poles (winter / summer) and its corresponding imagery (demonic / apocalyptic).[35]

Since the Renaissance, controversy surrounding the notion of dramatic genre has centred on interpretations of Aristotle and other ancient commentators. The most consistent position taken was the "rule" that the genres should not be mixed and that "tragicomedies," for example, were inferior works.[36] The next most important and agreed upon criteria was that of **decorum**, which, based on class, dictated that a character's appearance and behaviour must conform to that which was "natural," that is, according to class, age, gender and occupation. The romantics were the first to

---

[34]Aristotle, *Poetics*, chap. 2, 1448a, 1-20.

[35]Frye, *Anatomy*, Third Essay: "Archetypal Criticism."

[36]Giovanni Battista Guarini, however, made an atypical argument in favour of a possible mixture of tragedy and comedy in his essay, "Compendium of Tragicomic Poetry," 1599, in Dukore, *Dramatic Theory and Criticism*, pp. 150-156.

systematically revolt against the strict separation of genres and adherence to decorum.

Perhaps the most notable argument against genre in modern times was made by Benedetto Croce, who claimed that the notion of genre was totally arbitrary and abstract—that is, not related to actual practice, and therefore *post facto*.[37]

GESAMTKUNSTWERK

(German: "total art work") Specifically a term adopted by Richard Wagner (1813-83) to describe the theory and inspiration behind his "music dramas" in his essay, "The Purpose of the Opera."[38] The idea of the total art work, however, did not originate with Wagner, but with the humanist artists of the Italian Renaissance, who, in their attempts to develop modern versions of Greek drama, promoted theories about the aesthetic relationships between the arts in terms of shared or analogous principles (see **figure 12**). These efforts produced principles of **rhetoric** which cut across artistic lines. The end result of their investigations and experiments (in service to courtly and merchant patrons) was **opera**.

Wagner himself merely expressed prevailing romantic notions of the arts and their interrelationships, with theatre being the "meeting place" of them all. Recently, from the related perspectives of structuralism and **semiotics**, the relationship between artistic modes has focused more closely on modal interaction--the characteristics of aural, visual and kinetic communication (see **multi-modal communication system**). Such questions as the following need to be pursued further:

1. What are the relationships between sound, image and motion?

2. What is the relative strength (in audience perception) of sound, image and motion?

---

[37]Benedetto Croce, *Aesthetic*, trans. by D. Ainslie (London: Oxford Univ. Press, 1904).

[38]Richard Wagner, "The Purpose of the Opera," in *European Theories of the Drama*, Barrett H. Clark, ed., revised by Henry Popkin (New York: Crown, 1965), pp. 219-256.

3. Are there visual equivalents of sounds, visual equivalents of movements, aural equivalents of movements? Is there any validity to **"synaesthesia"** or *ut pictura poesis*?

4. How do varying rates of decay affect impact? That is, in a multi-modal event such as a play, stage settings last for relatively long periods of time, movements vary from the fleeting to the violent and individual sounds have very little duration at all.

5. What is the effect of the simultaneous transmission of sounds, images and movements? How does the principle of **synergy** apply to simultaneous transmission?

6. Can these modes be presented in a shifting hierarchy, that is, with sound, for example, being foregrounded momentarily, then movement, then image)?

(See E.T. Kirby, *Total Theatre*, 1969.)

GESTUS

This is a complex aesthetic / dramaturgical concept with major implications for **epic theatre** production (see **figure 9**). On one level it is Brecht's term for the central *social idea* of a scene or play (*grundgestus*). *Gestus* and *grundgestus* can thus be thought of as Brecht's equivalent of Aristotle's **action**. The social idea is performed as a crystallizing stage picture (**tableau**) or focused moment; the play as a whole illustrates an over-arching social statement.

On another level, *gestus* refers to all such "social gestures" which illustrate the underlying social implications of a scene or moment, as when a servant bows to his master in an acknowledgement of class superiority.[39] This implies that characters and scenes are conceived and performed more in terms of their social attitudes than their personal or scenic **objectives**, which also implies a shift away from characters' inner lives and toward their social behaviour--or at least toward the tension between

---

[39]Bertolt Brecht, "A Little Organon for the Theatre," in John Willet, ed. and trans., *Brecht on Theatre* (London: Methuen, 1964), pp. 190-220.

the two. Character *choices* and their implications are therefore paramount to Brecht's theatre.

(See John Willet, *Brecht on Brecht*, B. Brecht, *Sinn und Form,* 1950; 1964; John Fuegi, *Bertolt Brecht: Chaos According to Plan*, 1987; Elizabeth Wright, *Postmodern Brecht*, 1989.)

GIVEN CIRCUMSTANCES

Used by Stanislavsky to refer to all of the information embedded in a text which describes the environment and social context of the characters and their situation, including anything pertaining to previous actions which affect characters in the present (**exposition**).[40] In preparing a role as an actor, or a text as a director, or a setting as a designer, given circumstances are vital information. However, extreme care must be exercised when considering any information contained in **stage directions**.

GLORY

Any scenic device depicting the "heavens;" a favourite scenic practice of baroque scene designers of court spectacles and opera (e.g., Buontalenti). Glories typically included gods and goddesses from classical mythology seated on a semi circle of clouds.

GOTHIC

That period of cultural history bounded roughly by the 12th to 14th centuries, but limited in most of its manifestations to northern Europe. The influence of the gothic style, however, extended much further geographically and much later historically, as seen, for example, in the Canadian Houses of Parliament in Ottawa or St. Patrick's cathedral in New York.

---

[40]Constantin Stanislavsky, *An Actor Prepares,* trans. by Elizabeth Reynolds Hapwood (New York: Theatre Arts Books, 1941); see also Francis Hodge, *Play Directing,* 3rd ed. (Englewood Cliffs: Prentice Hall, 1988), chapter 4.

The French gothic style, which led the way, was principally an architectural style. Gothic church architecture, for example, exhibited several significant features which emphatically set it apart from the **Romanesque** style of the south, not least of which were higher, lighter naves, a greater area of glass (and thus more interior light), pointed arches and vaults.

The other arts at the time were analogously gothic in style: music, painting, sculpture, literature, and theatre were all affected by a new spirit of confidence in the life of this world and all served to bear testimony to a "heaven on earth." Gothic painting, up to and including the Van Eycks, was characterized by a meticulous observation of nature, as though God's presence was manifest in every detail; gothic music was *composed* (not improvised or learned by rote) in a polyphonic style and incorporated folk melodies; gothic drama, as exemplified by the Wakefield *Second Shepherd's Play*, was relatively realistic in style and naturalistic in the characterization of *individuals*, with a vernacular speech tuned to the characteristics of social class.

(See Arnold Hauser, *The Social History of Art*, v. 2, 1951; Johann Huizinga, *The Waning of the Middle Ages*, 1954; Barbara Nolan, *The Gothic Visionary Perspective*, 1977; Umberto Eco, *Art and Beauty in the Middle Ages*, 1986.)

GROUNDLING

Spectators forced to stand around a stage (or in the "pit" in the Elizabethan public theatres). Conflicting scholarship as to the demographics of the groundlings range from descriptions of an undisciplined rabble to a perceptive and appreciative middle class. The composition of Shakespeare's audience is of obvious importance to reception dramaturgy.

GUIGNOL

(French: *guignon:* "evil fortune") A term originally referring to children's puppet theatre in the 19th century, *guignol* (specifically *"grand guignol"*) has come to signify violence and horror in melodrama.

H

HAMARTIA

(Greek: "error," i.e., in judgement) For centuries Aristotle's description of the best possible plot for a tragedy--one whose hero's misfortune comes from some "error in judgement"--was used as a basis for a "tragic flaw" theory.[41] While an error in judgement or a mistake hardly points to a moral flaw in character, combined with the concept of *hubris* (pride), it is clear how such an interpretation could be made. But very few of the extant tragedies support either of these notions. In some of these plays, such as *Oedipus*, the hero tragically makes a mistake based on ignorance, and it is the **dramatic irony** of this mistake and its terrible consequences which produce the tragic effect.

Nevertheless, the argument persists that a hero who sets himself apart from his community and/or who attempts to circumvent his destiny has made a fatal error. In all of the discussion of the "tragic flaw" and *hamartia*, however, Aristotle is clear that the downfall must come from an act of the character--it is something he causes, not something done to him.

HAMATSA

The central action of the Kwakiutl winter dance drama cycle of coastal British Columbia. Dating from the 17th century, the *Hamasta* is probably the most theatrically sophisticated cycle of plays indigenous to North American native

---

[41]Aristotle, *Poetics*, chap. 13, 1453a, 5-15.

cultures.[42] Comparable to medieval **mystery cycles** in length and complexity, the *Hamatsa* cycle employs elaborate costumes, spectacular masks of the spirit world, drums, chanting and mime dances. Performed in ceremonial long houses during the winter months, the *Hamatsa* and other dramatic cycles are performed in conjunction with tribal *potlaches*.

HAPPENINGS

These are events in which improvisation, chance and direct audience participation are major factors. Happenings derive from two principle sources, the **avant garde** visual arts and **dada**. They flourished in the 1960's, along with **environmental theatre** and **Fluxus**. According to Michael Kirby, Happenings were "non-matrixed" events, that is, events structured by chance, non causal juxtaposition and the performance itself, with performers who could not be considered "characters" in the traditional sense.[43] Strong ties with visual arts meant that Happenings foregrounded the visual channel through dramatic images, rather than text based character relationships (see **tableau**). Happenings were thus the immediate predecessors of **performance art** and the **theatre of images**. Perhaps the penulti-mate Happening was the "bed in" (*Give Peace a Chance*) staged by John Lennon and Yoko Ono at the Queen Elizabeth hotel in Montreal (room 1742, June 1st, 1969) attended by friends and foes, the famous and curious, artists and media. (See Allan Kaprow, *18 Happenings in 6 Parts*, 1968.)

HERALD

Dramaturgically, the herald functions as a narrator of events occurring offstage and/or as an announcer for characters about to enter. Derived from the

---

[42]Peter L. McNair, "Kwakiutl Winter Dances," in *Arts Canada: Stones, Bones and Skin, Ritual and Shamanic Art*, Volume XXX, nos. 5 and 6, pp. 94-114.

[43]Michael Kirby, *Happenings: an Illustrated Anthology* (New York: Methuen, 1966).

"nuntius" in Greek tragedy (such as the messenger in *Oedipus*), the herald makes it possible to telescope otherwise lengthy activities which are incidental to the main **action**. In *Oedipus*, for example, the nuntius describes the horror of Oedipus' self-mutilation. By placing this in the narrative mode, Sophocles not only saves time near the end of a play which must rush to its conclusion or lose its tragic rhythm, he also prevents the blinding from becoming **anti-climactic**. The **climax** and **turning point** of the action have been passed by this time. Had the blinding been staged, the horror might have been more graphic, but it would have superseded the true climax. The **action** of the play is not self-mutilation, but self-discovery.

HERMENEUTICS

(Greek: the study of "interpretation") Medieval drama, theatre and performance cannot be interpreted strictly as literature or drama, nor can the meaning of its lines, images and movements be taken at face value. To the medieval mind, every element in the hierarchy of heaven, earth and hell, every moment in "history," is endowed with divine significance. This means that the semantic, syntactic and even the pragmatic "meanings" of each sign (see **code**) are multi-layered. Thus in medieval hermeneutics, the major levels of interpretation were interdependent and simul-taneously present:

1. the **literal:** the meaning of the individual sign in its everyday communicative sense (necessary as a base in human experience);

2. the **moral:** the sign's didactic function in terms of human behaviour; thus, an act on stage, or a choice made by a character, has moral implications and its function was to teach right from wrong;

3. the **allegorical:** the sign's allegorical implications--the principle of personification as a level of meaning for those (in the audience) who have enough knowledge and intelligence to make connections between the concrete and the abstract. This level, considered in combination with the previous two, results in a basic interpretation of the text which is consequently shown to have more than a superficial or merely functional meaning;

4. the **typological:** (see **figura**) this level requires a corresponding level of knowledge of the Bible and its official interpretation; typology is concerned with direct connections between the Old Testament (as prophesy) and the New (as fulfillment): the events, persons and objects in the Old prefigure events, persons and objects in the New;

5. the **anagogical:** this is the most sophisticated and esoteric level of interpretation. Anagogy implies a mystical relationship between the earthly and the divine, between things of this world and the world to come.

Taken together, these five levels of interpretation give a dramatic text, such as the Wakefield *Second Shepherd's Play*, a profundity its surface or literal level alone only hints at. Since the audience at the performance of a mystery cycle was a cross section of medieval society, all levels of meaning would not be accessible to every member, but each would enjoy the performance according to his or her level of cultural literacy. By extension, hermeneutics can apply to the interpretation of any text.

(See Arnold Hauser, *The Social History of Art*, v. 2, 1951; Johann Huizinga, *The Waning of the Middle Ages*, 1954; Edgar de Bruyne, *Esthetics of the Middle Ages*, trans. by E.B. Hennessey, 1947, 1969; Barbara Nolan, *The Gothic Visionary Perspective*, 1977; Umberto Eco, *Art and Beauty in the Middle Ages*, 1986.)

HERO

The central character, the **protagonist**, the chief **agent** of a play's **action**. It should be noted that the central character may be a woman; nevertheless, the overwhelming male dominance in drama (historically) presupposes a hero as the driving force of an action. Notable exceptions, ironically, begin with the Greeks: for example, *Antigone, Electra, Medea, Lysistrata*, etc.

HEROIC DRAMA

An English form of tragedy, written in heroic couplets during the Restoration period and influenced by French **neoclassicism**. The typical action involved members of the court and aristocracy in conflicts of love, duty and honour. It was a short lived form and particularly susceptible to parody (see *The Rehearsal*, 1671, by George Villiers; see also Arthur C. Kirsch, *Dryden's Heroic Drama*, 1965; John Loftis, ed., *Restoration Drama*, 1966).

HUBRIS

(Greek: "insolence") To behave as though one were above natural laws as they apply to all mortals. The term also forecasts the fall which will inevitably follow from such behaviour. This "tragic flaw" theory of the downfall of a tragic hero is probably neoplatonic in that it facilitates a Christian interpretation (the sin of pride) of an ancient concept. It is not used in this sense in Aristotle, nor does it really apply to most Greek tragedies (see *hamartia*).

HUMOURS

(See **comedy of humours**) One of the areas of ancient theory uncovered by humanist scholarship and employed in Renaissance drama. Essentially a theory of human behaviour (and thus of significance in creating characters), the four fundamental *humours* (sanguine, phlegmatic, choleric and melancholic), were thought to be related to an excess of a corresponding fluid in the body (blood, phlegm, choler and bile). References to "the humours" and a particular character's humour abound in Elizabethan drama, from Shakespeare's Jaques in *As You Like It* to Jonson's *Everyman in His Humour* and *Everyman Out of His Humour*.

According to this scheme, a *sanguine* personality is cheerful and hospitable, generous and righteous; a *phlegmatic* personality is lethargic and easy going; a *choleric* personality is quick tempered and vengeful; and a *melancholic* personality is depressed and withdrawn.

I

ICONOGRAPHY

(Greek: ikon, *"image"*) The study and/or knowledge of specific meanings attached to pictorial representations.   Christian iconography, for example, is concerned with the complex interplay of esoteric symbolism in visual depictions of the life of Christ and the teaching of the gospels. In the Renaissance and Baroque periods, western art (and theatrical scenery, costumes and properties) became even more complex in its synthesis of Christian and classical iconography.

In **semiotics**, an icon is one of three forms of **sign** (icon, index and symbol); one which creates a relationship between signifier and signified by inherent similarity, for example, a statue of a horseman is an icon because it is similar to a man on horseback and it signifies cultural and/or social supremacy.

ILLUSIONISM

The attempt to create in the viewer or audience the feeling that what they are witnessing is real, but not necessarily the same actuality as their own. (See **realism.**) Since most viewers understand that the work is in fact not real, the **convention** requires a "willing suspension of disbelief" (Coleridge).

IMITATION

(Greek: mimesis, "to mimic or copy") Imitations are simulations of reality-- however that reality is defined. One of the central tenets of art and one of the most controversial notions in aesthetics is the question: to what extent does art copy life, and in what sense do we use the word "life" (i.e., physical, emotional, intellectual, spiritual)? From the perspective of Plato's "Ideal," to what extent is art an imitation of an imitation, that is, how do we know that (empirical) life is real?

"Art as imitation" has many philosophical problems attached to it, and as a consequence it has had different implications for different cultures, from Greek idealism to Shakespeare's "to hold a mirror up to nature," for example. How a society defines and represents reality, in other words, is a key to an understanding of its culture.

(See Erich Auerback, *Mimesis: Representations of Reality in Western Literature*, 1946/1953; Susan K. Langer, *Feeling and Form*, 1953.)

During the Italian Renaissance, *imitatio* was a central tenet of the "rhetoric of beauty" in humanist neoplatonism (see **figure 9** and **neoclassicism**). *Inventio, dispositio, ethopoea* and *expressio* were all related critical principles in the analysis of the various arts and in comparisons of one art with another (***ut pictura poesis***).

(See Paul Oskar Kristeller, *Renaissance Thought and its Sources*, 1979; Michael Baxandall, *Giotto and the Orators: Humanist Observers of Painting and the Discovery of Pictorial Composition, 1350-1540*, 1971.)

The rejection of "art as imitation" in avant garde and **modernist** art has been a mark of alternative, as opposed to traditional art. The idea that art does not attempt to imitate anything, real or ideal, has had profound effects on theatre, if not drama (see **performance art**).

The notion of mimesis has also been applied to technological change and popular culture. Old, familiar forms of architecture and ceramics, clothing and modes of transportation, sports and entertainment are perpetuated in the forms of the new: the "station wagon," for example, was originally made partially of wood in imitation of earlier forms of horse drawn beach wagons for the wealthy. One of the reasons for this (universal) phenomenon, apparently, is to cushion the shock of the new. (See Alan Gowans, *Learning to See: Historical Perspectives on Modern Popular/Commercial arts*, 1981.)

IMPERSONATION

Imitation of a very specific kind: pretending that one is someone (or something) else; adopting a "mask," or fictional persona. Impersonation lies at the heart of **drama**, not necessarily **theatre** or **performance**, in that characters, who are fictional, serve as agents of an **action**.

Purists would maintain that to "act," that is, to adopt a role, is to physically, emotionally and intellectually imitate another person--even if that person is one's own creation. In practice, many actors have merely shaped the character as drawn by the playwright to fit their own personalities and physical characteristics. At various times in the commercial theatre, this is what was meant by being a "star" as opposed to a being a "character actor."

(See Viola Spolin, *Improvisation for the Theatre*, 1963.)

IMPRESSIONISM

A term derived from the painting style of the late 19th century, especially in France, impressionism denotes a concern for how objects actually appear to the eye as opposed to how they should appear in their isolated purity. The affects of light and shade, of reflected colour from nearby objects, the shimmering effects of sunlight through the air--all condition the actual appearance of things. Consequently, painters took their easels into the field in order to capture fleeting moments or "impressions" of nature--and by extension, any subject. Coupled with this close, objective look at nature was a new appreciation of colour: how various tones "mix" in the eye of the beholder and how a shadow cast over part of an object will change its colour.

In drama and theatre, impressionism did not formally have followers, but the work of a few playwrights, notably Chekhov, comes close to a dramaturgical equivalent. In the *Cherry Orchard*, for example, Chekhov presents his audience with flurries of **french scenes** in which fleeting impressions are given of different character combinations: fragments of their conversations, incoherent thoughts and frustrated emotions. This is done with apparent objectivity and an attention to fine detail. Over the course of the play we become familiar with the nuances of individual characters' personalities as they relate to each other, and we are reminded that **drama** is above all *human relationships in crisis*. In this process, Chekhov defines **tragicomedy** for modern times. While individual characters cannot see themselves and their problems with any objectivity (and are consequently self centred and self pitying), we in the audience can sympathize with them and laugh at them simultaneously. Chekhov brings his scattered impressions into focus for the audience, much in the same way that there is a focal point for viewing a painting by Seurat: stand too close and you are overwhelmed by dots of colour, back up and the whole comes together.

IMPROVISATION

Improvisation is the essence of artistic creativity. It means both spontaneous creation and free embellishment: spontaneous in that the improvisation is conducted without specific planning (*extempore*) and embellishment in that the improvisation is always a response to or an ellaboration of an existing thing, idea, theme, event, etc.

In an important sense, all art is improvised: within certain constraints of medium, materials, **conventions**, patronage and/or subject, an artist creates something new. Improvisation is the artist's survival skill; without it the work is merely derivative and imitative. This was the fundamental precondition of the successful **commedia** actor or troupe: regardless of the number of preplanned *lazzi* it was the actor's ability to improvise, to respond *extempore* to others on stage, which guaranteed his success. As the level of improvisation declined in the commedia, the form began to die. Similarly, in the world of jazz, it was the black slave's ability to "roll with the punches" and come up laughing, to improvise on the white man's music (and on each other's), that his life and his art depended.

Consequently, if a performance is to maintain its appearance of spontaneity and if a performer is to maintain his reactive relationship with the audience's shifting moods and his fellow actors' free embellishment, improvisation must remain a central acting skill. This is true regardless of how tightly the play has been scripted and rehearsed. Each performance contains an essential element of improvisation and in the live theatre **presence** is practically a defining condition.

INCITING MOMENT

In Gustav Freytag's scheme, this is the incident or act which begins the **action** of the play. While this term designates the initial act of the **plot**, it is the **point of attack** which locates the act structurally within the **fable**. (See **Freytag's Pyramid**.)

INCIDENT

(See **plot**)

INDEX

In **semiotics**, one of three forms of **sign** (index, **icon, symbol**), which creates a relationship between signified and significr--in this case through a causal connection. For example, the painted "index finger" which points to a door or the presence of smoke, which is an index of fire.

INDICATING

Acting without substance; "ham" acting. Indicating an emotion or intention without being involved produces a performance which is superficial at best and insincere or inconsistent with the character at worst and thus a performance which is unbelievable.

INGENUE

An innocent young woman *type* of character; an actress who plays such roles.

IN MEDIA RES

(See **ab ovo**)

INNAMORATA(O)

(Latin: "lover") The hero and heroine (unmasked) in a **commedia** scenario, with names such as Lilio and Isabella.

INTERLUDE

(Latin: "between play") A short piece (not necessarily dramatic) inserted between the acts of a play or between the main entertainments. Specifically, the English Interlude of the 16th century was a short play to be performed by boys between the courses of a banquet. Frequently these Interludes were little more than dramatized debates with a moral, if serious, or punch line, if comic. In terms of **social function**, Interludes marked the transition from an ecclesiastic to a courtly culture.

(See **Intermezzo**. See also, Henry Medwall, *Fulgens and Lucrece*, ca. 1497; John Heywood, *The Four PP*, 1560.)

INTERIOR MONOLOGUE

Unlike the literary interior monologue, in theatre the term refers to the thoughts, images, plans etc. which go through a character's mind and which provide a basis for his **objectives**. The theatrical interior monologue, in other words, is an *actor's construct*, an aid to developing and playing a role.

INTERMEZZO

Generally, a piece inserted between the acts of a longer dramatic work (see **Interlude**). Specifically, an *Intermezzo* was a musical **tableau** inserted between the Acts of a comedy or **pastoral drama** enacted at the Italian "palaces" during the Renaissance (see **figure 12**).

Intermezzi were usually staged by humanist scholar/artists of the Italian *camerata*. Their typical function was celebratory: that is, the occasion of their performance was usually an important court celebration--a wedding, a treaty, the birth of an heir etc. In their development through the 16th century, *Intermezzi* became increasingly elaborate, both musically and scenically. Musical forms, such as **recitative** and **aria**, which could carry dramatic content were being developed; perspective scenery, using a **proscenium arch** became a vehicle for elaborate displays of humanist **iconography** and **rhetoric**.

As celebratory **multi modal communication systems**, *intermezzi* were among several forms of **festive theatre** undergoing radical change through the Renaissance and Baroque periods (see **masque,** *ballet de coeur*). All of these forms, under humanist guidance and promotion, were attempts to recapture and revitalize classical Greek theatre for contemporary court needs. By the turn of the century (i.e., by 1597), these prototypes had become **opera**.

Perhaps the most elaborate *intermezzi* to be staged in the late Renaissance were those celebrating the wedding of Ferdinand de Medici, Grand Duke of Tuscany in 1589.[44] Eight intermezzi, designed by Buontalenti and performed by members of the Florentine Academy (*camarata*), were staged between Acts of a comedy (*La Pellegrina*, by Bargagli) which was performed by the renouned **commedia** troupe, I Gelosi. This *intermezzi* team, essentially, was responsible for the development of early opera (e.g., *Daphne*, by Peri and Rinuccini in 1597). The team, headed by Giovanni Bardi, humanist scholar and producer, included Buontalenti (designer), Rinuccini (librettist), Cavalieri, Peri, and Caccini (composer/performers).

(See A.M. Nagler, *Theatre Festivals of the Medici*, 1964; Roy Strong, *Splendour at Court: Renaissance Spectacle and Illusion,* 1973; Arthur R. Blumenthal, *Theatre Art of the Medici*, 1980.)

ISSUE

Dramaturgically, the content or subject of a specific **beat** can best be described as an underlying *issue between characters*, as this places emphasis on the

---

[44]Arthur R. Blumenthal, *Theatre Art of the Medici* (Hanover: Univ. of New England Press, 1980), p. 1.

developing human relationships of the drama. An issue is the basis of the **subtext** of a character relationship and it is fuelled by each character's **objectives**. The question to be asked in script analysis, therefore, is: "what is *at issue* between these characters at this moment? The follow-up question, logically, is: "what is the relationship between this issue and the **action** of the play as a whole?" Questions like these are of particular interest to directors; actors are more interested in questions like: "how does this issue affect me, or, how important is this issue to me?"

To find issues in a text, one must focus on the shortest complete drama-turgical unit: not the **french scene**, which may contain several issues, but the **beat** and begin with the topic of conversation between characters. What are they talking about? What do they mean by what they say, that is, what is really *at issue between them?* Issues are by no means always momentous; many merely facilitate the plot. But each scene usually has at least one central issue at stake and analysis must identify this and relate it both to other issues and to the action as a whole.

J

JESSNERTREPPEN

Named after the German director, Leopold Jessner (1878-1967), who belonged to the Max Reinhardt "school" of staging and who was a leading proponent of German **expressionism**. His rejection of **representational** scenery led to experiments with levels and ramps and specifically with massive flights of stairs.

JIG

An afterpiece in Elizabethan theatre; part of the **revels** at a **masque**; a folk dance and/or song; a satirical performance by a few clowns.

JO-HA-KYU

From Japanese aesthetics; specifically, from the *Noh* theatre theories of Zeami Motokiyo (1363-1443), *jo-ha-kyu* is a rhythmic progression, from slow and dignified to lively and long to fast and short movements. To Zeami, this pattern was natural, that is, a part of nature's rhythm, and thus was the underlying rhythm of all aspects of life. Insofar as Art attempts to imitate nature, Art should have *jo-ha-kyu* as its foundation.[45] *Jo-ha-kyo* is the foundation of the Noh's rhythm; it is also structural in that each unit of the Noh performance is based on the same pattern, from the traditional five Noh play cycle to the individual plays and even scenes within

---

[45]Zeami Motokiyo, *Kadensho*, trans. by Chuichi Sakurai, et al (Kyoto: Sumiya-Shinobe, 1968), pp. 39-40; 104.

each play. Each of these units is seen to have three structural phases: introduction, development and resolution. The tripartite structure is the essence of the Zen Buddhist philosophy which informs Noh and all Japanese aesthetics. *Jo-ha-kyu* is thus related to the three stones in a Zen garden and three pines of the Noh stage which symbolize (variously) "heaven," "earth," and "man." (See also *yugen, aware, sabi.*)

There are several cross cultural echoes of Japanese aesthetics in western theatre, music and dance. The basic sonata form, for example, is similar to *jo-ha-kyo*: *Allegro* (sometimes preceded by a slow introduction), *Adagio, Scherzo* and back to *Allegro*. **Freytag's Pyramid** has rhythmic implications in its structure, expecially in its proportions (short, long, short), and various commentators have noted comic and tragic "rhythms."[46]

JORURI

(See *Bunraku*)

JOURNAL

Artists' journals, diaries, "commonplace books" and sketch books have a long and venerated tradition. Several have been published: Defore's *Journal of the Plague Year*, Peyps' *Diary*, Bysshe's *Art of English Poetry*, and Leonardo's sketch books are famous examples. Depending on the art, journals are tools for recording observations and ideas for later use and for working out plans for more formal work. In the theatre, the **performance text** and **prompt book** are (or were) journals of a kind and actors have long used journals to record character analyses, ideas for rehearsal, observations of people and so on.

---

[46]In addition to Frye (*Anatomy*), see Langer, *Feeling and Form*, chapters 18, 19 and Fergusson, *An Idea of the Theatre*, chapter 1, pp. 25-27.

JUVENILE

A young, innocent, male character type; an actor who is usually cast in such roles. (See **ingenue**.)

K

KABUKI

(Japanese: *ka* "song," *bu* "dance," *ki* "skill") The 17th century popular Japanese theatre. The *Kabuki* is a derivative form: it first appeared as a low, sensuous and bawdy prostitute's entertainment; next as a "poor man's" *Noh* (the public was excluded from court entertainment); then as an imitation of *Bunraku* (puppet) performance style; finally emerging with its own style as a popular romance or melodrama.

Several stages of censorship and regulation followed *Kabuki's* development, in effect forcing it to become acceptable middle-class entertainment. (Note that in England, at roughly the same time, middle class theatre was developing through similar formal and regulatory and commercial influences; in France, popular "speechless" theatre became mime during the 18th century in response to government censorship.) One of the stylistic effects of the regulations in Japan, for example, was the *onagata*, or female impersonator, adopted when women (and thus the original prostitutes) were barred from the public stage.

In contrast with the *Noh*, the *Kabuki* is a spectacular form of entertainment, with much action and elaborate scene and costume changes. In place of the *Noh* masks, *Kabuki* actors wore stylized makeup. Its relationship to the puppet theatre, however, gave *Kabuki* its characteristic acting and movement style. Performers' movements imitated those of puppets, their voices were similar to *Bunraku* chanters and their costume changes were executed on stage by handlers dressed in black.

(See Earle Ernst, *The Kabuki Theatre*, 1956.)

KATHAKALI

(Hindu: derived from Kali, goddess of destruction and Shiva, lord of the dance) A classical Hindu dance-drama based on the *Mahabharata* and *Ramayana* epics.

KYOGEN

A word which designates both a type of satirical farce (and comedy) and a performer--both associated with the 15th century *Noh* court theatre of Japan. The form and content of the *Kyogen* plays, in contrast to the *Noh,* are much more "realistic."

The *Kyogen's* association with the Noh bears an interesting aesthetic and functional similarity to the relationships between Greek tragedy and the **Satyr** play and the **masques** of Ben Jonson. "Comic relief" does not adequately describe this function, since the relationship is more organic. The *Kyogen,* satyr and **anti-masque** all provide a counter message, style, mood and function to the more sublime *Noh,* tragedy and masque. There is also an ideological dimension to these relationships, since all three forms were associated with lower class performers, stories and attitudes. The contrast between the lofty and the low, therefore, served to reinforce the legitimacy of the elite class.

L

LAZZI

(Italian: "jeer, mock") A memorized speech or line of business or virtuoso display of a **commedia dell'arte** actor--his stock in trade. ("Line of business" refers to the characteristic behaviour of stock characters.) These *lazzi*, in contrast to the improvisational nature of the performance in general, were not only memorized, they were perfected routines appropriate to the actor's character (**mask**), inserted into the performance at opportune moments. Here the actor could display his skill while defining his character. Successful actors, such as the Andreinis of the I Gelosi, had many such *lazzi* they could use whenever necessary, and their fans expected it.

LEGITIMATE THEATRE

Specifically a term indicating the licensed theatres in England after the Restoration which were the only ones licensed to present traditional drama. Pirate theatres got around these restrictions by inserting musical and/or dance numbers in their shows. This practice led to hybrid forms of "music hall" entertainments such as **vaudeville, pantomime, melodrama** and so on. Generally, the legitimate theatre referred to spoken, as opposed to musical drama.

LEHRSTUKE

(German: "teaching play") A form of didactic play developed by Bertolt Brecht and Erwin Piscator and the composers of *das neue musik* of the 1920's in Germany. The **social function** of the *lehrstuke* was to teach the common man, through organizations such as the **workers' theatre**, the realities of post was politics and economics.

The form and style of the *lehrstuke* have been compared to various kinds of medieval drama, such as the **morality** and **mystery** play, whose character types represented abstract ideas and/or social forces rather than unique individuals.

(See George H. Szanto, *Theatre and Propaganda*, 1978; Erwin Piscator, *The Political Theatre*, 1978.)

LIBRETTO

(Italian: "little book") The text of an opera or other form of **music theatre**. The *libretto* includes both the dialogue and lyrics of a musical comedy, the words of the **recitative, arioso** and **arias** of an **opera**.

NOTE: in the creation of a work of music theatre, the relative importance of words and music has been a major dramaturgical consideration throughout the history of both music and **festive theatre**. If an existing *libretto* is put to music, for example, the resulting **action**, characters and **plot** are likely to be more complex than if the music has priority from the beginning. Conversely, while most successful operas are very complex and profound musically, their *libretti* are relatively simple--an indication that musical ideas and structures dominated the creative process.

LINES OF BUSINESS

(See *lazzi)*

LITTLE THEATRE

(Community theatre; amateur theatre) The little theatre movement in America began in response to the independent theatre movement in Europe: alternative theatres such as the *Theatre Libre*, the Independent Theatre, *Die Freie Buhne*, the Abbey theatre and others. In the United States, little (non-professional) theatres such as the Washington Square Players and The Provincetown Players led the way, but by 1925 "nearly 2,000 community of little theatre companies were registered with the Drama League of America. . . ."[47] In Canada, the Little Theatre Movement began about a decade later in reaction to the American and British influence over Canadian theatre. The Dominion Drama Festival, an annual event for the best amateur theatre in the country, was held every year until 1969. While many Little Theatres in both countries mounted mainly commercial hits from New York and London, several led the way in producing the best of modern European drama along with original and experimental works. (See **alternative theatre**.)

LITURGICAL DRAMA

Drama inserted into the liturgy of the church service which developed out of musical embellishments (**tropes**) of the text. These little playlets, which were sung, were intended to illustrate key moments in special **masses**, such as Christmas and Easter.

(See the *Quem Quaeritis* of the *Regularis Concordia*, c. 975 at Winchester; see also, Glynne Wickham, *The Medieval Theatre*, 3rd ed. 1987; Arnold Williams, *The Drama of Medieval England*, 1961.)

LIVING NEWSPAPER

An offshoot form developed by the **Federal Theatre Project** in the United States during the depression, although it originated in the **expressionist** movement in the early 20's. The **social function** of Living Newspapers was to make the theatre relevant to large audiences of ordinary people (many of whom were unemployed) by dramatizing the day's newspaper headlines with sketches, songs and improvs: for example, *One Third of a Nation*, 1938 (i.e., one third were unemployed at the time), which dealt with slum housing. As such, the form belongs to the **documentary theatre** genre. Historically, and from the perspective of social function, Living Newspapers also belonged to the **Workers' Theatre Movement**. By 1939 Congress

---

[47]Brockett, *History of the Theatre*, p. 627.

refused to continue funding for the project, but by that time theatre in the United States had been revitalized and was on its way to its "golden age."

(See John O'Connor and Lorraine Brown, eds., *Free Adult, Uncensored: The Living History of the Federal Theatre Project*, 1978; Halle Flannagan, *Arena: The History of the Federal Theatre*, 1985; Malcolm Goldstein, *The Political Stage: American Theatre and Drama of the Great Depression*, 1974.)

LOBBY

(See "production dramaturgy" under **dramaturgy**) While we might take the lobbies of theatres for granted today, they are a relatively modern invention added to theatre architecture in response to changing theatre-going customs in the 19th century. "Lobby" is here used to indicate an architectural complex of spaces and functions: the "foyer" (entrance space, with box office ticket windows), lobby (waiting area, with cloak room) and lounge (refreshment area, with seating and washrooms).

Lobbies may be configured differently in different theatres, but their functions are integral to audience enjoyment (even perception) of a production. The audience not only has to be out of the weather while waiting for tickets, have a place to wait for friends and to put coats, they must also have a place to realx and have refreshments during intermissions. The latter, incidently, ties the structure and length of a play to the architecture. Consequently, the layout, area per (auditorium) seat and amenities of lobbies are important considerations to theatre architects and managers.[48]

---

[48]Harold Burris-Meyer and Edward C. Cole, *Theatres and Auditoriums* (New York: Krieger Publishing, 1975).

M

MANSION STAGING

(Biblical: "My Father's house has many mansions.") A medieval form of simultaneous staging, with several "mansions" ("stations") or sub-settings placed on a long platform, around a town square or banquet hall, or in procession. The empty spaces in between and/or in front were dramatically neutral (see **platea**). In the staging of a **mystery cycle** or **passion play** these might include God's throne on one side, "hell mouth" on the other and a variety of stations between the two poles. Mansion staging was superseded by the **thrust stage** in England and the **proscenium** stage with perspective scenery in Italy. (NOTE: the *Ballet Comique de la Reine*, France, 1581, employed both mansion and proscenium staging in the same banquet hall.)

MASK

The subject of masks in the theatre has profound aesthetic, cultural and historical dimensions. Since **theatre** involves **performance**, the performer's face (and body) is the prime vehicle of visual communication. As such, it could be argued, the face of a performer is a changing **sign** as well as a "persona." It can also be argued that all of us act all of the time in our social relationships.[49] How the individual presents him/herself in a family situation is quite different from the self presented to a prospective employer, for example.

---

[49]Erving Goffman, *Presentation of Self in Everyday Life* (New York: Doubleday, 1959).

The performer's face, throughout history (and cross culturally) has been modified with many forms of masks, from varying degrees of makeup to constructed half and full coverings (made from a variety of materials) representing fantastic or mythic personae to common individuals. Four dramaturgical considerations arise with such modifications: first, the relationship between the performer and his/her mask; second, the relationship between the mask and the material (e.g., the script); third, the relationship between one mask and another; and fourth, the relationship between the mask(s) and the audience. Each of these problematic areas has many variables and significant implications. For example, does the performer try to "become" the mask, or does he/she maintain a strong degree of neutrality? Does the performer change his/her voice and physical expression to suit the mask or is the mask allowed to make its own statement? Is the mask a stylized, but organic outgrowth of the script or is it a specific *interpretation*? Do masks relate to each other as individuals or as types (i.e., does the presence of masks preclude **realism**)? Is the audience's perception of the mask intended to be fixed or is individual subjective response to be encouraged through the power of suggestion, by the play of light across the mask at different angles or by changing situations and relationships? On the level of semantics, does the mask represent a clearly known type of character (such as **Arlecchino** in the **commedia** in which the mask attains the function of an **icon**), is it intended to be mysterious or is it to have a variety of possible connotative meanings?

Masks in the theatre have also facilitated certain kinds of staging. In the ancient Greek theatre, for example, the use of masks made it possible for males to play female roles and for one actor to play more than one role. Masks have also facilitated mass communication through size and shape: this may have been a consideration in the large Greek ampitheatres by boosting the visual message; it has certainly been an asset in other kinds of performance to large crowds, such as the Bread and Puppet Theatre and several oriental theatrical styles.

(See Libby Apel, *Mask Characterization*, 1982.)

MASQUE

(See **figure 12**) The word is etymologically related to "mask" and historically related to folk entertainments involving disguise. The masque may in fact have been related to the **mummers' play**, since both involved holiday "visitings" and festive entertainment in which the spectators or hosts joined in the fun.

The masque proper, however, was originally a court celebration in honour of Tudor events and accomplishments. Allegorical scenic devices and **pageants** used in outdoor tournaments were wheeled into the court's banquet hall to serve as a focus for the evening's entertainment. Often this consisted of little more than a short allegorical mime performed by disguised courtiers, possibly a song and a celebratory poem or two, climaxed by dances or **revels** between the masque performers and the ladies of the audience.

In Elizabeth's time the masque was further developed as a distinct art form, but remained just one of several theatrical celebratory forms of her reign--the others being the Accession Day tilts, allegorical displays and masque-inspired plays by leading playwrights (such as Shakespeare's *A Midsummer Night's Dream*, 1595).

The peak of the masque's development was reached under the patronage of King James I and especially his queen, Henrietta, between 1603 and 1625. (Compare the French court's *ballet de cour* and the Italian *intermezzi*.) During this period, the masque became a major spectacle, with scenic designs by Inigo Jones (who brought Italian perspective scenery to England), texts by leading playwrights such as Jonson, Chapman and Beaumont, and music by Chapman, Ferrabosco, Campion and others. Commissioned for special celebrations of the court, the Jacobean masque was by now a lavish *dramatic* event, with a central **action**, characters, plot and conflict--the latter provided by the **anti-masque**, an invention of Ben Jonson's. All masques had a celebratory **social function**, in which the wisdom and accomplishments of the Godly Prince were praised. Typically, the action of a masque followed a pattern: peace and order, threatened disorder (the anti-masque) and the restoration of peace and order.

The characters were either allegorical or drawn from classical mythology and they were played by courtiers in disguise. (The anti-masquers, also disguised, were played by professionals.) Regardless of the masque's lavishness, however, the climax of the celebration occurred with the unmasking and the revels.

(See Stephen Orgel, *The Jonsonian Masque*, 1965, and *The Illusion of Power: Political Theatre in the English Renaissance*, 1975.)

MASS

(Latin: *missa, mittere*, dismissal) The Christian Mass, developed by the early church fathers between AD 600 and 1000 in celebration of the Eucharist. The Mass has long been acknowledged as **ritual theatre** and drama, with performers and audience, a plot which reaches a climax (holy communion), costumes, properties, music and a theatrical setting. Amalarius, Bishop of Metz during the reign of Charlemagne, described the Mass to the "*simplicores*" as a ritual drama with all the participants as role players.[50] In the 10th century the Mass was the setting and the occasion of the emergence of **liturgical drama**.

More profoundly, and ultimately of more relevance to the character of ritual drama, Roland Murphy, S.J., has analyzed the Mass from a "biogenetic structural perspective."[51] In this analysis, each section of the Mass, from the "Rite of Entry" to the "Dismissal" is discussed in terms of its contribution to the psychic unity of the individuals in the congregation. The essential difference between this ritual drama and **theatre** is not so much belief as psychic or **aesthetic distance**.

MEANING (in the theatre)

"Meaning" in art, as in life, is a slippery proposition. The problem lies with

---

[50]"*De ecclesiatics officiis*, in O.B. Hardison, *Christian Rite and Christian Drama in the Middle Ages* (Baltimore: Johns Hopkins, 1965), pp. 37-79. See also, Dom Gregory Dix, *The Shape of the Liturgy* (London: Daire Press, 1946).

[51]"The Mass: a Ceremonial Ritual," in *The Spectrum of Ritual: a Biogenetic Structural Analysis*, Eugene G. d'Aquili, ed. (New York: Columbia Univ. Press, 1979), pp. 318-41.

imprecise modes of communication, whether language, image, sound or gesture--all are merely approximations of intent. The reason for this is not simply the **ambiguity** at the core of language, the problem also lies with the subjective *self* which attempts to use these modes to communicate with objective *others*:

> Even on the rare occasions when word and gesture happen to be valid expressions of personality, they lose their significance in their passage through the cataract of the personality that is opposed to them. Either we speak and act for ourselves--in which case speech and action are distorted and emptied of their meaning by (the other) or else we speak and act for others--in which case we speak and act a lie.[52]

In the theatre, which is a **multi-modal communication system**, this problem is compounded immeasurably by the ambiguity of each channel and by the multiple interpreters involved in the production, from playwright to actors, director and designers. Then, to make matters worse, the audience is composed of individuals whose understanding is only partially shaped by collective references. Little wonder that the control of such ambiguity is one of the primary functions of the director!

MELODRAMA

(See **figure 1: "The Ur Drama, Summer,"** and **figure 12**) A form of drama (with music, originally) which developed out of the French Revolution in response to the promotion of the middle class to economic and political leadership in at least France and England. Historically and dramaturgically, the form derives from the medieval **morality** in that its purpose and methods are didactic and its characters are so simply drawn that they approach the level of allegory.

As entertainment, a melodrama exploits sensational action at the expense of serious thought and character; it typically features suspenseful curtain scenes, or a structure based on a series of climaxes leading to a final confrontation between "Good" and "Evil;" originally, a melodrama also featured spectacular scenery as well

---

[52]Samuel Beckett, *Proust* (New York: Grove, 1957), p. 46.

as scenes with songs and dances--all devices intended to heighten emotional response. A melodrama can usefully be considered a sub genre of **festive theatre** wherein middle class values are renewed and the victory of the Good is celebrated.

As a middle class morality, therefore, it is important that a melodrama end happily: the Good are rewarded and the Evil punished (see **poetic justice**). In this respect, at least, a melodrama is generically akin to comedy (see Northrop Frye, *Anatomy of Criticism*, 1957). However, whereas in comedy the ultimate objective is fertility and renewal, in melodrama it is the triumph of virtue which is celebrated. As a result, the typical melodrama foregrounds the threat of evil--in the character of the **villain** and his henchmen--and the consequent danger to the innocent. Since innocence triumphs over evil by acquiring knowledge and experience, melodrama, like comedy, is a **displacement** of a "rite of passage" (see **comedy**). The struggle of the hero and heroine against the villain is a moral test.

As the preferred entertainment of a large and wealthy middle class, melodramas were not only morally acceptable, they were enormously popular and as such contributed to the schism between the romantic **avant garde** and the popular commercial arts of the 19th century. At the same time, melodrama contributed to the growing demand for **realism** as a style of theatrical presentation: the new audience wanted to see their own lives and life styles on stage. This meant heavily furnished drawing rooms, contemporary costumes and real props.

The major creator of melodramas in France was Guilbert Pixerecourt (e.g., *Coelina*, 1800, adapted in English by Thomas Holcroft two years later as *A Tale of Mystery*); and in England Dion Boucicault (e.g., *The Corsican Brothers*, 1852).

(See James L. Smith, *Melodrama*, 1973; Peter Brooks, *The Melodramatic Imagination*, 1976; Eric Bentley, *Life of the Drama*, 1965.)

METATHEATRE

Webster's dictionary supplies a guide to the use of the "meta" prefix: ". . . used with the name of a discipline to designate a new but related discipline designed to deal critically with the original one."[53] When applied to theatre, it is a **modernist** term describing a "self conscious theatre," or "theatre about theatre" (see Pirandello's *Teatro sul Teatro*, 1922). It is not enough, however, to assume that this merely means that an audience is made aware that it is watching a play--that is, through an anti-illusionist strategy (see ***verfremdungseffekt***). Rather, a metatheatrical code will call attention to itself as being deliberately *theatricalized*. The purpose of this strategy is to expose and thus critique the theatrical **conventions** of the work. In the modern theatre, Luigi Pirandello was the first to create *meta plays*, with *Six Characters in Search of an Author*, 1921, being the most well known. Since that time several playwrights have exploited the conventions of the metatheatrical style, notably, Tom Stoppard (*Rosencrantz and Guildenstern are Dead*, 1967, *The Real Inspector Hound*, 1968, *Jumpers*, 1972) and Michael Frayn (*Noises Off*, 1982).

Such codes are by no means limited to modern theatre. The Renaissance and especially Baroque theatres, for example, abounded in self-reflecting devices, such as the "play within a play" convention (see the "Mousetrap," *Hamlet*, III, 2) and diverse comparisons of life, drama and the stage (see Calderon's *The Great World Theatre*, 1645, and *Life is a Dream*, 1636).

(See Lionel Abel, *Metatheatre: a New View of Theatrical Form*, 1963.)

METHOD

An early American version of the "Stanislavski System" of actor training based on an incomplete and misunderstood reading of his theories as found in his *An Actor Prepares* (1936) and *Building a Character* (1949). Many of these misconceptions, including Stanislavski's own revisions were clarified in his *Creating a Role*, 1961, but by this time the American "method" had been modified through experience.

---

[53] *Webster's Ninth New Collegiate Dictionary*, Frederick C. Mish, ed. (Springfield: Merriam-Webster, 1983), p. 745.

Associated with the early years of the Group Theatre and the Actor's Studio under the direction of Lee Strasberg and Elia Kazan, the method emphasized inner development, the **interior monologue, motivation** and character biography--often at the expense of performance technique. The method was also a response to the American penchant for **realism** and **naturalism**. It was not as useful for other styles of production or characterization.

(See Robert Lewis, *Method or Madness?* 1960; Lee Strasberg, *Strasberg at the Actors' Studio*, 1965.)

MIE

(Japanese: ***Kabuki* theatre**) The *mie* is the climactic pose (visual **code**) of the *Kabuki* actor, held for up to 20 seconds to crystallize the conjunction of character, situation and attitude. For example, the entrance of the warrior hero down the *hanamichi* is halted at the half way point for such a pose, while the villain on stage hurls curses and taunts at him. The *mie*, as performed, is a complex **sign** involving the combined functions of **index, icon** and **symbol**, depending on one's perspective.

The *mie* is not an exclusive **convention** of the *Kabuki*, however. The Greek theatre performance employed poses of characters and chorus (*cheironomia*) to signify and underscore known social attitudes (such as exclusion); the 19th century theatre, especially in English and American **melodrama**, employed individual poses and group **tableaus** for similar purposes (see Tom Robertson's *Caste*, 1867).

MILES GLORIOSUS

(Latin: "braggart warrior") Comic type from Greek **new comedy** and Roman comedy; generic ancestor of *Capitano* in the **commedia** tradition (see *alazon*) and countless other cowards, from Falstaff to the Cowardly Lion in *The Wizard of Oz*.

MIME

(a) Ancient comic sketches of folk material which possibly influenced early

Greek and Roman comedy; (b) "speechless theatre" of 18th and 19th century France--a method of circumventing prohibitions against popular or non-academy theatre;[54] (c) theatre which relies soley on movement, gesture and facial expression (with the possible addition of properties) as its communication modes.

Since language has been the main vehicle for the communication of ideas, the elimination of speech from the actor's means has forced the remaining two channels (visual and kinetic) to compensate, with corresponding adjustments made by spectators. The result has been a theatre which foregrounds those aspects of human experience which are non-conceptual, emotional, intuitive and above all *inferential*, that is, mime relies on the power of suggestion and the ability of a viewer to "fill in the blanks." Silent films are excellent illustrations of these principles: those which do not require projected captions being the most successful.

MIMESIS

(See **imitation, impersonation**)

MINSTREL SHOW

19th century American "music hall entertainment" which originally employed white performers in black faced imitation of African American stereotypes. The minstrel show evolved from very simple, but popular shows by three or four performers to large companies (see the E.P. Christy Minstrels of the 1850's). Minstrel shows typically followed a pattern of formal introduction (the "walk around"), song and dance specialties (interwoven with jokes) and dramatic sketches. Important stars of the American musical stage, such as Stephen Foster, Scott Joplin, Eddy Cantor and Al Jolson, were trained within the minstrel tradition.

---

[54]Frederick Brown, *Theatre and Revolution* ((New York: Viking, 1980), pp. 41-82.

MIRACLE PLAY

A non-liturgical medieval play concerning a specific biblical event and/or the life of a saint.

MISE EN SCENE

(French: "put in the scene; on stage; staging") A staged text; the director's, actor's and designer's interpretations of the playwright's embedded codes. Sometimes refers merely to the physical setting. The *mise en scene* is the subject of **performance dramaturgy**.

MIXED MEDIA

(1) In visual art, the mixture of found objects, paper, wood etc., with paint (the "collage"); (2) in the theatre, the mixture of live with recorded elements, such as slides, film and sound.

MODELLBUCH

(German: "model book") Neither a **prompt book**, nor a **performance text**, the *modellbuch* is specifically a record of a production's rehearsal period--as developed by Bertolt Brecht in his work with the Berliner Ensemble. *Modellbucher* with hundreds of photographs have been published (e.g., B. Brecht, *Couragemodell*, 1949). Their purpose was to serve as adjuncts to Brecht's dramaturgical theories and as guides to future productions. Brecht learned the importance of such records when he worked as Max Reinhardt's assistant. Each photograph, as a frozen moment in the performance, also serves to illustrate the concept of **gestus**.

MODERN DRAMA

Usually understood to have begun with the plays of Henrik Ibsen (1828-1906) and August Strindberg (1849-1912) in that their collective works introduce the variety of artistic styles generally associated with the arts of the modern world, from

realism and **naturalism** to **symbolism** and **expressionism.** Modern drama thus begins with the later phases of the romantic period and signals the advent of the **avant garde** and its split from popular commercial art on the one hand, and academy art on the other.

MODERNISM

A generic term used to categorize similar stylistic techniques and aesthetic strategies in all of the arts from ca. 1875 to ca. 1955. (See **aestheticism, art for art's sake.**) Some or all of the following characteristics are generally included:

1. The art is self consciously analytical, with a strong tendency toward abstraction: the real subject of art is art itself. For example:
    --in painting, the characteristics of the medium become the subject of the work (i.e., paint, colour, brush strokes, mass, line etc.), as do the characteristics of human sight and visual communication (e.g., cubism);
    --in fiction, the characteristics of story telling (narrator, reader/listener, printed words/spoken words, plot, point of view etc.) intrude into the story, with the result that the reader becomes acutely conscious of the writer's effort and technique (see Samuel Beckett's *Watt*, 1944, 1953);
    --in music, the characteristics of sound (musical and non musical) and aural communication are elements of compositions which explore the phenomenon of human hearing (e.g., the compositions of John Cage);
    --in dance, the characteristics of the human body in motion--in defiance of gravity--are celebrated through leaps, spins and poses and through the coordination of arm and leg movements and body relationships (e.g., the works of the modern pioneers, such as Martha Graham, Merce Cunningham);
    --and in theatre, the characteristics of **impersonation** and **performance**, **presence** and **illusion** are exploited with the willing collaboration of an audience (e.g., Pirandello's *Six Characters in Search of an Author*).

2. An effort by the artist to make the viewer more fully aware of the act of viewing, listening, imagining, empathizing etc.

3. To comment on the relationship between art and life; between the

art experience and the life experience; between creativity and living.

4. To "distance" the commonplace in an effort to indirectly comment on its value and "meaning" (e.g., Andy Warhol's soup cans).

Modernist theatre, which includes **metatheatre, absurdism, happenings** and **performance art**, thus exploits the principles of **dramaturgy** to fulfill the above objectives.

In terms of content, modernist theatre in various ways provides the audience with an ironic perspective or a consciously collaborative perspective on the characters--their relationships, the issues between them, their situation--and on the overall action. As a genre, for example, **tragicomedy** is modernist in its ironic perspective.

MONOLOGUE

A speech of some length and formality (see **soliloquy, aria**), but with others on stage.

Loosely, this term can refer to any longish speech spoken while alone or in the physical presence of others. This raises problems, however: can others on stage hear this speech (if so, what is their response and how can the prefix "mono" apply; if they cannot, does the audience know this--i.e., is a monologue an extended **aside**)? What then is the difference between a monologue and a **soliloquy**?

This term has also been used in connection with an audition piece, that is, a ' speech taken from a scene in a play and performed out of context.

MORALITY PLAY

A vernacular, secular play written in an allegorical style; a non-liturgical medieval play in an allegorical style whose purpose was to teach a moral and/or spiritual lesson.

Dramaturgically, the allegorical style had a profound influence on later

Renaissance drama as a crude, but effective method of characterization and of generating conflicting **issues** (e.g., "Good Deeds" versus "Pride").

The morality was an effective vehicle for the education of a largely illiterate community and it was thus a tool for the propagation of secular ideology as well as religious doctrine. Abstract ideas (e.g., Justice), qualities (e.g., Mercy), generalized types (e.g., Merchant) and functionaries (e.g., messengers) and so on were personified and placed in dramatic conflict. The **climax** occurred and the moral was spelled out when the forces of Good triumphed.

Moralities flourished during the formative years of medieval society and well into the Renaissance. The form influenced many later types of drama, including **epic theatre, expressionism** and **melodrama**. A fundamental reason for this is that since **theatre** is a communal event, its function has usually been not only to entertain, but also to teach. The history of **drama** and theatre in terms of **social function** is thus a history of a pendulum swing between these two not necessarily competing objectives.

Possibly the two most well known examples of the form in the English language are *Everyman*, Anon., ca. 1500 and *The Castle of Perseverance*, Anon., ca. 1425. These two examples also illustrate the two basic styles of **performance dramaturgy** employed by medieval moralities.

In the Netherlands, "Chambers of Rhetoric" were humanist debating societies interested in the performing arts. In the 16th century dramatic contests were held in which plays written as allegorical moralities competed on given secular themes.

(See Robert A. Potter, *The English Morality Play: Origins, History and Influence of a Dramatic Tradition*, 1975.)

MOTIVATION

The sociology of human behaviour argues that people act out of a complex of drives including social conditioning and desire.[55] In acting theory, largely shaped by Stanislavski, his followers and 19th century determinism, research into a character's biography and social circumstances will provide the reasons for his/her behaviour in any scripted situation. This is the "push" theory of behaviour which tends to focus on the past (i.e., on "motivation"); a counter proposal emphasizes the "pull," namely character *objectives*, or intentions, which focus the actor's attention on the character's future. (See Robert Cohen, *Acting Power*, 1978).

Character motivation, the creation of **interior monologues** and the development of detailed character biographies and psychological profiles are legitimate areas of actor research for those plays with serious actions and well developed characters in the tradition of **realism** and **naturalism**. Comedies, farces and **presentational** styles of theatre, however, benefit much less from such work.

MULTI-MODAL COMMUNICATION SYSTEM

Any communication system which simultaneously employs more than one channel or "mode" benefits from a form of **synergy**. The theatrical event is a multi-modal communication system which employs aural, visual and kinetic channels. (**Music theatre** is a particularly complex **MMCS** since each of the three channels has a variety of expressions: speech, songs, instrumental music, sound effects; costumes, settings, properties, lighting; gestures, movements, dances. Another complex form is **mixed media**, in which slides, film and recorded sound are added to live performance.) These systems are synergistic if their channels are organized in a shifting hierarchy throughout the performance, otherwise they could compete to the point of incoherence or "static." Such hierarchies typically foreground one channel and use the others as supportive background, as when lyrics and musical accompaniment support a dance number. Another strategy is to shift between modes

---

[55]Erving Goffman, *The Presentation of Self in Everyday Life* (New York: Doubleday, 1959).

by temporarily suspending one or more channels (as when movement stops during an important speech). (See Kier Elam, *The Semiotics of Theatre and Drama*, 1980.)

The MMCS is not only synergistic, it also produces communicative redundancy, as on at least one level the messages sent to an audience are duplications of each other in different forms. For example, the emotion of a line between lovers, an embrace, musical underscoring and a shift in lighting--all occurring at the same time--support the central action of the scene. One important implication of synergy and redundancy for dramaturgical theory, therefore, is that the *relationships between the arts* in a MMCS become as important as each of its components.

Roland Barthes has called the theatrical event, "a kind of cybernetic machine," with a density of signs and sign systems found nowhere else in human communication and as such it is a major challenge to semiotic analysis.[56]

MUMMER'S PLAY

A medieval folk play performed by amateurs in disguise on special occasions, such as Christmas. Mummers typically performed in village squares, in front of and even inside people's houses for "treats." A mummer's play might include yuletide songs, folk dances, pagan sword dances and a ritual drama involving a battle, death and resurrection--all symbolizing or promoting renewal. In England, under the Tudors, such plays were often called St. George plays after the patron saint, who appears as the play's hero.

(See E.K. Chambers, *The Medieval Stage,* 2 vols., 1903.)

MUSIC THEATRE

(See **figure 12**) (a) Used as a generic term, music theatre embraces all forms of theatre in which music plays a significant part in the structure of the **action**.

---

[56]Roland Barthes, *Critical Essays*, trans. by Richard Howard (Evanston: University of Illinois, 1972), pp. 261-62.

Opera, operetta, musical comedy and even some of Brecht's **epic theatre** are forms of music theatre. (b) "Modern" music theatre tends to be nearly or completely through composed like opera, but involves small casts, simple settings and current subject matter.

(See Leonard Bernstein's *Trouble in Tahiti*, 1952; Gian Carlo Menoti's *The Medium*, 1954; B. Brecht and Kurt Weill, *Die Kleines Mahagonny*, 1930.)

MUSICAL COMEDY

(See **figure 12: "The Ancestry of American Musical Comedy"**) A sub category of both **festive theatre** and **comedy** in which music and dance are major components, but which also includes spoken dialogue. Modern musical comedy became a genre in its own right with such shows as *Showboat* (Hammerstein/Kern, 1925), *Oklahoma!* (Hammerstein/Rodgers, 1943) and *The Music Man* (Wilson, 1957). In the new form, music and **libretto** were fully integrated with character and action; songs and dances were not arbitrarily placed, but were expressions of the emotion of the moment and actually advanced the action.

(See Gerald Bordman, *American Musical Theatre, a Chronicle*, 2nd ed., 1992; Richard Kislan, *The Musical: a Look at the American Musical Theatre*, 1980.)

MYSTERY PLAY (CYCLE)

One of several plays in a cycle performed in celebration of the Feast of Corpus Christi, a festival proclaimed by successive Popes in 1264 and 1311, but which did not become universal in the west until the 14th century. While the religious function of the festival was a celebration of the Eucharist, the **social function** became an expression of the social and economic power centres of medieval urban life, with major participation of the clergy, the guilds (both trade and craft) and the town.

The **action** of the mystery cycle was to demonstrate the redemption of mankind through the triumph of Christ over Satan as foretold in the Old Testament and fulfilled in the New. A cycle was thus a collection of many short plays or

pageants, each illustrating a story from the Bible--theoretically beginning with the Creation story (from *Genesis*) and ending with incidents from *Revelations*. In England, such cycles include the York (48 extant plays), Chester (24 plays), Wakefield (32 plays) and Coventry (42 plays)--all dating from the last half of the 14th century. In Europe, even larger cycles have survived, but these tend to focus on the life or *passion* of Christ--hence **Passion Play**.

Serious analysis of the **dramaturgy** (textual, performance, production and reception) of the mystery cycle began after the second world war. It was with these studies (prompted by several productions) that the great complexity of the cycles was appreciated: that is, not just their length, but also their variety of dramaturgical styles and **conventions**. Profoundly spiritual scenes were mixed with broad parody, farcical elements were interjected into traditional biblical scenes, **representational** elements and scenes alternated with, or were interrupted by **presentational** moments and so on.

(See Glynne Wickham, *Medieval Theatre*, 1987; Alan H. Nelson, *The Medieval English Stage: Corpus Christi Pageants and Plays*, 1974; Jerome Taylor and Alan H. Nelson, *Medieval English Drama: Essays Critical and Contextual*, 1972; V.A. Kolve, *The Play Called Corpus Christi*, 1966.)

MYTH

(See **figure 1: "The Ur Drama"**) A narrative about beginnings; stories about the "magic time" (see Mircea Eliade, *The Myth of the Eternal Return*, etc.); a culture's collective beliefs which underlie specific doctrines and ideologies and traditions; "one of the four archetypal narratives, classified as comic, romantic, tragic and ironic."[57] Myth becomes important in drama with **displacement**, or adaptation to more sophisticated demands, just as **ritual** is displaced by **theatre**. (See also, **Ur Drama, legend, displacement**.)

---

[57]Northrop Frye, *Anatomy of Criticism*, chapter 2.

N

NARRATIVE

Story telling: an account (either of fact or fiction) of events usually of the past. Narrative presupposes a *narrator*, which gives the story a **point of view**. Narrative can be (and often is) employed as a dramatic or theatrical **convention** in a number of ways. A character might tell a story to other characters; a narrator may address the audience with commentary and background material; a character may simply recount an incident from the past (i.e., **exposition**); or a character may employ narrative as a **tactic** to achieve a personal **objective**.

All of these uses of narrative (and others) can be important because they provoke a different mental response in the audience (**reception dramaturgy**). When dialogue is used as a function of future oriented objectives in the present, the audience is engaged in constant anticipation; but when narrative is used, the audience mentally relaxes into a more passive state, contemplating images of the past evoked by the character / narrator. Finally, theatre is **presence**, and its activities are conducted in the here and now; narrative is imaginative and its activities are conducted in the past, that is, in the mind. (See W.T. Mitchell, *On Narrative*, 1981, a collection of essays on the aesthetic implications of the narrative mode in a variety of contexts.)

NATURALISM

There has been a tendency to equate (and thus confuse) naturalism with **realism**, especially in literary and art criticism. In drama and theatre (or textual and performance dramaturgy), realism is a *style* of writing and performance, while naturalism is a *theory* of human behaviour. As such, naturalism provided a basis for the development of dramatic characters, whereas realism provided a style for their depiction and presentation. While the road to realism proceeded via several routes through the 18th century, naturalism was inspired by the "sociological" theories of August Compte (*The Course of Positive Philosophy*, 1830) and by Darwin's *The Origin of Species*, 1859, which demonstrated the function of heredity and environment in the behaviour and development of species. Consequently, while a play such as Tom Robertson's *Caste*, 1867, with its box set and attempt to create an illusion of actuality, but with stereotyped characters is an example of early realism, Ibsen's *Hedda Gabler* has naturalistically conceived characters who are presented in a realistic style.

NEOCLASSICISM

Generally, a humanist movement of the Italian Renaissance which spread throughout Europe (especially in the 17th century), neoclassicism was a *program* intended to fulfill several interdependent functions:

1. A reconciliation of Christian doctrine and faith with classical mythology and philosophy (called "neoplatonism:" see **figure 9**);

2. an attempt to recapture and revitalize with neoplatonic idealism the arts of classical Greece and Rome;

3. in the process, an attempt to develop *prescriptive* rules of **rhetoric** which would apply to all arts;

4. to place the arts in the service of the "Godly Prince," the patron, in an "alliance with power;"[58] in other words, to use the arts as vehicles of conviction and persuasion--propaganda for an ideology of

---

[58]Lauro Martines, *Power and Imagination: City States in Renaissance Italy* (New York: Knopf, 1978), p. 205.

absolutism.[59]

The Florentine *camarata*, founded in the mid 15th century by Marcilio Ficino (who developed the contemporary version of neoplatonism) and followed nearly a century later by Giovanni Bardi, was responsible for turning humanist philosophy into theatrical experiments leading to **opera**. To the humanist scholars and artists of the academy, drama and especially theatre were exemplary arts for several reasons: first, theatre encompassed the other arts; second, drama not only had a classical model (Greek Tragedy), it also had a classical theory (Aristotle's *Poetics*); third, theatre, as a public event, could be broadly useful in the celebration and promotion of the Medici family. Much time and effort were therefore expended in the academy to develop a Renaissance equivalent of Greek tragedy.

The rhetorical rules of neoclassicism, as applied to theatre, stemmed from the basic assumptions of Ficino's neoplatonism, namely, that all observable phenomena are mere reflections of Reality, but that the human mind can "know" the Real. Accordingly, it was the function of the arts to mediate between everyday phenomena and the Ideal. Art should thus be "true to nature" (**verisimilitude**) by imitating universals, not particulars. Consequently, characters in drama should not behave as individual people might behave in actuality, but as they ideally should behave (**decorum**). Drama should be true to nature by observing the **unities** of time, space and action; **tragedy** and **comedy** were "pure" genres and should not be mixed; the function of drama was to reveal the universal principles behind the passing particulars of life and thus to serve as models of bahaviour and idea.

Neoclassic doctrines of art were highly influential in Europe as long as the ideology of absolutism could be maintained. Consequently, "establishment" theatre was a theatre sanctioned by humanist academies and controlled by court bureaucracy. Rejection of neoclassicism came with the rise of the middle class to economic and political power during the 18th century. In the arts, this radical shift began with

---

[59]Alan Gowans, *Learning to See*, chapter 5.

romanticism and continued in the **avant garde**.

(See Paul Oskar Kristeller, *Renaissance Thought and its Sources*, 1979; for translations of most relevant documents, see Allan H. Gilbert, ed., *Literary Criticism: Plato to Dryden*, 1967.)

NEW COMEDY

(See **old comedy, middle comedy**) A term used to differentiate Roman comedy from Greek (Aristophanes) and Hellenistic (Menander). While the essential **action**, being an archetypal or generic pattern, remained *renewal*, and the subjects dealt with were still sex and power, sterility and ridicule, the form, style and character types changed radically. Moreover, these changes were a response to new political, economic and social realities--as style changes in art always are.[60] The following are the major characteristics of new comedy:

1. New comedy focused on the typical exploits and domestic concerns of middle and lower class characters;

2. character types predominated: that is, there were no specific references to or characters drawn from actual contemporary people. Included were the miserly father (**senex**), the braggart warrior (**miles gloriosus, alazon**), the wayward / lost / destitute brother / sister / child and the tricky servant;

3. dramatic structure was typically a pattern of **prologue** followed by five acts; situations typically involved young love and/or blocked inheritance; and all ended happily, with the old being ridiculed and the young triumphing;

4. scenic elements indicated typical domestic or commercial streets with as many doors as possible (usually three, plus exits to other parts of town).

5. there was no chorus; there were asides and soliloquys, but little direct address; there were many opportunities for mime and comic business; the language was close to the vernacular.

---

[60]Alan Gowans, *Learning to See*, pp. 490-94.

(See George E. Duckworth, *The Nature of Roman comedy,* 1952; Erich Segal, *Roman Laughter: the Comedy of Plautus,* 1968; R.L. Hunter, *The New Comedy of Greece and Rome,* 1985.)

NEW STAGECRAFT

The dominance of **realism** as a style of theatrical performance and production dramaturgy In Europe and America were seriously challenged by the freedom inspired by controllable electric light and a parallel rejection of **naturalism** on the part of playwrights of the **avant garde**.

The new stagecraft movement was led by Adolphe Appia (1862-1928) and Edward Gordon Craig (1872-1966). Their theories and designs demonstrated a non-illusionistic, abstract conception of theatrical space. Instead of imitation trees, the atmosphere of a forest; in place of realistic rooms, suggested interiors and generalized props; instead of streets, functional ramps and platforms.

(See Adolphe Appia, *The Work of Living Art,* 1921 (1962); Lee Simonson, *The Stage is Set,* 1932; Denis Bablet, *The Theatre of Edward Gordon Craig,* 1966; Richard C. Beacham, *Adolphe Appia,* 1987.)

NOH

(Japanese: "talent") *Noh* is the classical Japanese court theatre which flourished during the Muromachi period (14th -15th centuries). Its two founding artists, Kan'ami (1333-1384) and his son, Zeami (1363-1444) brought *Noh* from its rather primitive origins in agricultural dances to a highly sophisticated and esoteric form of ritual theatre. The *Noh* is a stylized non-illusionistic, but representational theatre performed by both masked and unmasked characters, an unmasked chorus and musicians. It is performed on a bare stage with a few very suggestive **properties** and elaborate, colorful costumes. In terms of its performance and production dramaturgy, therefore, the *Noh* can be compared with some of the characteristics of both the Greek and Elizabethan theatres.

There are two types of characters: the *Waki*, who is unmasked and whose function it is to introduce the situation and to provide the audience with a point of view and "bridge" to the mystery of the main character and the heart of the play's **action**; and the *shite,* who is usually masked and who is the focus of the play. While the *Waki* is usually of this world, the *shite* often represents a figure from the past in disguise. Both may have followers as companions or servants.

The writings of Zeami (see the *Kadensho,* translated by Sumiya Shinobe, 1968) are the major source of *Noh* aesthetics and dramaturgy, including methods of training--all permeated with the Japanese synthesis of Zen Buddhism and Shintoism. Since the *Noh* was court sponsored and performed exclusively before Japan's elite class, and since very few companies were licensed to perform, the art and technique were handed down through families of performers. These factors tended to result in a very rigid form of performance: archaic gestures, language and speech rhythms and a slow, ritual-like pace. In many of these respects, the *Noh* is quite different from the **Kabuki,** which was intended for a more popular audience.

For western theatre, the importance of the *Noh,* especially at the time of its discovery by European artists (post 1867), was that it came as a liberating revelation to playwrights, designers and directors who felt stifled by **realism** and **naturalism.** All of the arts of the west, from painting to acting were profoundly influenced by such a radically different culture and aesthetic.

(See Donald Keene, *Noh: the Classical Theatre of Japan,* 1965; Faubion Bowers, *Japanese Theatre,* 1974; Kunio Komparu, *The Noh Theatre: Principles and Perspectives,* 1983.)

NUNTIUS

(Latin: "messenger") A character in Greek drama whose function it is to relate events of **offstage life** and to introduce characters appearing from offstage. The *Nuntius* was therefore a *structural device*, making it possible to exclude certain violent or horrible deeds from the stage and to summarize events which would prolong the play and detract from the main **action.** The messenger who appears at the end of *Oedipus*, serves these functions.

O

OBJECTIVE

The goal a character intends to pursue in a **beat** or scene; the central or unifying **action** of a play (or scene); a character's *overall* goal ("super objective"--a term from Stanislavski's system). Scenes and beats are in fact structured by characters' opposing objectives. Objectives thus relate to both private agendas and the **issues** between characters.

An actor's job, in script analysis and rehearsal, is to identify these objectives and to make choices about how to pursue them--in terms of specific **tactics** and an overall **strategy** (which are both modified by on-going circumstances). It is through these choices that actors create characters.

(See Robert Benedetti, *The Actor at Work*, 1990; Robert Cohen, *Acting Power*, 1978; Uta Hagen, *Respect for Acting*, 1973.)

OBLIGATORY SCENE

(*Scene a faire*) A scene or confrontation between characters which the playwright prepares for and leads the audience to expect. This may be, for example, the **recognition** scene or the **climax**. Dramaturgically, the obligatory scene is part of the apparatus of suspense in that it is an anticipated scene.

OBSTACLE

If a character has an **objective**, but nothing stands in his way, his achievement is hardly dramatic; obstacles are threats to the attainment of one's objective and they are usually provided by other characters who have conflicting objectives. This is why **drama** is defined as "human *relationships* in crisis."

OFFSTAGE CHARACTERS

Characters who never appear on stage, but who nevertheless affect the onstage characters and thus the **action** of the play. For example, in Ibsen's *Hedda Gabler*, Tesman's Aunt Rena is one of two aunts who raised him. While she never appears, there are several references to her, a pair of slippers she embroidered for him are brought on stage (with mixed results), and when she is about to die in the final act, Tesman leaves as soon as he hears about it in order to be with her. Such characters are indirect agents and are consequently important dramaturgical tools for the playwright.

OFFSTAGE LIFE

This general term refers to a variety of dramaturgical techniques for creating an illusion of a continuum between the life on stage and off. The playwright does this with offstage dialogue and noises, with **embedded** references to offstage events, sounds, images and characters. A rock (or any other object, such as the boot in Chekhov's *Cherry Orchard*) thrown on stage and noted by a character is a manifestation of the existence of offstage life. (What about a rock thrown on stage and *not* noticed by anyone except the audience? This would affect the audience's perception of the play, but it could only occur through a **stage direction**.) A scene in the offstage kitchen between Martha and Nick in Edward Albee's *Who's Afraid of Virginia Woolf?* interacts with the onstage scene between George and Honey. Telephone calls from offstage not only influence those on stage, they are also indirect manifestations of offstage characters (see, for example, David Mamet's *American Buffalo*).

Two criteria must be met for an effective offstage life in most forms of **representational** theatre: first, instances must be acknowledged in the dialogue, which means, second, that offstage life must have some effect on the characters and action. The consequence of this is that a fundamental *relationship* between on and offstage life is created by the playwright with important significance in the overall meaning of the work.

OFFSTAGE SPACE AND TIME

The illusion that the stage space seen by the audience continues into the wings and that the events on stage exist in a temporal continuum extending beyond the beginning and ending of the play. Such an illusion, deliberately suggested by the playwright with **embedded** references, is a consequence of the illusion of **offstage life**. Embedded references to offstage time make time an agent of the action, just as references to offstage spaces, actions and characters are proof of their influence on the action.

The additional dramaturgical interest here is that the *relativity* of space and time becomes apparent. This relativity has been present in most drama, but perhaps never so consciously as a dramaturgical technique than in plays such as Ibsen's *Hedda Gabler* and Chekhov's *The Cherry Orchard*: the former as a high point of **naturalism** (character behaviour tied to environment and heredity) and **realism** (illusionistic staging); the latter as an ironic perspective on both naturalism and realism. In both plays, the specific settings and their geographical locations are conditioned by time and memory, and conversely, time is defined by the style and age of the settings.

OLD COMEDY

A generic reference to the type of Greek comedy of which only the plays of Aristophanes are extant. In contrast to **new comedy**, these comedies are characterized by:

   (a) elements of the fantastic (*Birds, Clouds, Frogs*);
   (b) references to current events;

(c) political satire and caricature;

(d) direct political opinions;

(e) a structure comprised of an initial problem, a "happy idea" (which is a proposed solution), and putting the happy idea into practice, which leads to a **climax**;

(f) a very important, involved chorus.

(See C.W. Deardon, *The Stage of Aristophanes*, 1976; Rosemary M. Harriott, *Aristophanes: Poet and Dramatist*, 1986.)

ONNAGATA

(Japanese: ***Kabuki***) A male actor trained to perform female roles in the *Kabuki* theatre. Women were barred from the stage in the formative period of the *Kabuki* on charges that they were prostitutes and thus unsuitable for the middle class audiences the theatre was trying to attract. The aesthetic of the *Kabuki* (and the *Noh* in this respect) depends on the heightened, artificial femininity produced by these virtuoso performers. In the *Kabuki*, the *Onnagata* creates an illusion of the female; in the *Noh*, the contrast between the female mask and costume and the obviously male actor is part of the aesthetic.

OPERA

(See **figure 12**) "Drama unfolding as much in the music as in the words."[61] Opera is a **displaced** form of a festival of renewal (see **festive theatre**). Historically, opera resulted from the efforts of Italian humanists during the late Renaissance to revitalize the form of Greek theatre as a vehicle for the celebration of their powerful patrons on special occasions. These efforts were prompted by the discovery of ancient texts and a desire to reconcile Christianity with classical philosophy (Neoplatonism). The major artistic problem they had to solve was a musical form for dialogue (**recitative**) which would be open ended and follow natural speech patterns.

Proto operas were festive wedding celebrations performed at court by artists

---

[61]Robert Donnington, *The Opera* (New York: Harcourt Brace Jovanovitch, 1978), p.1.

of the Florentine *camerata*, such as Bardi, Caccini, Peri and Buontalenti. These entertainments combined spectacular tableaus of classical characters, orchestral music and singing with a popular comedy (see **intermezzi**). The first operas, that is, the first unified, through composed musical dramas were *Dafne*, by Peri and Rinuccini in Florence in 1597, *Euridice*, by the same team (plus Caccini) and Monteverdi's *Orfeo* in 1607 in Mantua.

(See Robert Donnington, *The Rise of Opera*, 1981; John D. Drummond, *Opera in Perspective*, 1980; Donald J. Grout, *A Short History of Opera*, revised, 1973; Joseph Kerman, *Opera as Drama*, 1959.)

<u>OPERETTA</u>

(See **figure 12**) In the 19th century this term came to signify more than merely a short opera. The light, comic works of such composers as Johann Strauss (*Die Fledermaus*), Jacques Offenbach (*La vie parisienne*), Franz Lehar (*The Merry Widow*) and Arthur Sullivan (*HMS Pinafore*) are a few examples. Since these are full length works, the major dramaturgical difference between the operetta and **opera** was the spoken dialogue in most of the former.

Historically, and in terms of **social function**, the advent of the operetta signalled the growing influence of the middle class. Opera through the 18th century, and "grand opera" in particular, were arts of the aristocracy (and the social climbing upper middle class). Operettas were both "genteel" and light in form and middle-class in sentiment. In *HMS Pinafore*, for example, it is the aristocracy which is ridiculed and middle class sentiment which is upheld. In America, operettas were one of several strands in the development of **musical comedy** (e.g., Victor Herbert's *Naughty Marietta*).

P

PAGEANT

An ambiguous term which can refer to the wagons used to carry individual tableaus of medieval **mystery plays**, or to the plays and tableaus themselves, or to modern theatrical events which feature historical tableaus, songs, dances and skits, and which are performed as parts of holiday festivities. In all cases, pageants were often components of parades, and all are subsumed by **festive theatre**.

In the development of **opera** and **musical comedy**, scenic tableaus and major choral and dance numbers are **displaced** pageants. A series of such tableaus thus constitute displaced parades.

PANTALONE

A masked character of the **commedia dell'arte**; the *senex*, or old lecher/miser/despot; historically, Pantalone was a caricature of a Viennese merchant. Pantalone was usually the parent or guardian of the hero and/or the suitor of the heroine. As the major representative of the older generation in a **comedy**, Pantalone was the object of ridicule. Pantalone evolved in **displaced** forms throughout Europe in succeeding centuries. Characters such as Moliere's Miser and Gilbert's Sir Joseph (*HMS Pinafore*) are widely separated examples of the type.

PANTOMIME

A term with several historical applications, from a performer in ancient Rome to a 19th century form of English music hall entertainment; from the entertainment itself to the performers in them; from a **dumb show** to mime. Consequently, the term has become obsolete.

PARABASIS

(Greek: "to the side") In Greek **old comedy**, a formal section in which the chorus stepped out of the action momentarily to address the audience directly. The *parabasis* was also used structurally to divide the play into two quite distinct parts. Aristophanes used the *parabasis* to put forward his own political ideas and criticism and to plead his own cause. As such, the content of the *parabasis* usually had little to do with the play itself.

In terms of performance dramaturgy, the *parabasis* is an indication of the generally **presentational** style of old comedy (or of all Greek theatre?). It also testifies to the audience's acceptance of the two **conventions** existing in the same performance: both "here" and "not here;" "now" and "once upon a time."

PARASITE

A character type in Greek **new comedy**; a servant or slave (of the **trickster** archetype) who is always scrounging free meals and who can usually be bribed with food. **Arlecchino** in the **commedia** often has this as a character trait, as do many other comic characters through history. Sociologically, the existence of the type testifies to the low opinion middle class Romans in the audience had for servants. (See Plautus' *Menaechmi*; Terrence's *Phormio*.)

PARODOS

(Greek: "side passage") The passage on either side of the Greek theatre used as entrances by both chorus and audience (cf. the Roman *"vomitoria"*); also, the choral ode sung by the chorus during or just after its entrance.

From the perspective of production dramaturgy, the *parodoi* make a major visual statement and obviously link life on the outside with the drama on the inside in a way that an entrance "from the wings" does not. (See **chorus**.)

PASSION PLAY

A medieval **mystery cycle** of a scope limited to the "passion" of Christ, that is, the last days of his life--usually from the Temptation through the Resurrection. This, of course, conforms to the specific mandate of the Feast of Corpus Chrisit, to celebrate the Eucharist. The Passion presented every ten years at Oberammergau, Austria, continues the tradition.

PASTORAL DRAMA

(See **figure 1**) A genre (romance) from the Italian Renaissance about "arcadia," the secular version of the Garden of Eden. The form derives from classical Greek and Roman poetry, especially the ten *Bucolics* of Virgil. Part of Italian humanist efforts to revitalize classical culture, the pastoral drama was intended to be a neoplatonic version of the Greek **satyr play**.[62] Consequently, the pastoral drama was filled with classical allusions and was very much tied in with a revival of chivalry and courtly love.[63] Knights or courtiers, their ladies and servants would leave the evils of urban life for an idealized country setting to play at being simple country people (shepherds) while reading poetry to each other. Although largely imagined threats might intrude upon this Arcadia, the endings were invariably happy, although perhaps tinged with melancholy.

Essentially, the "pastorale" is a dramatic version of the romance archetype.[64] It had a profound effect on the literature, painting and theatre of all nations with absolutist ideologies. In England, especially, the pastorale and the mythos of Arcadia

---

[62]Oscar Brockett, *History of the Theatre*, p. 159.

[63]Frances A. Yates, *Astraea: the Imperial Theme in the Sixteenth Century* (London: Routledge and Kegan Paul, 1975), pp. 89-110.

[64]Northrop Frye, *The Secular Scripture: a Study of the Structure of Romance* (Cambridge: Harvard Univ. Press, 1976).

permeated the reign of Elizabeth I through poetry (e.g., Edmund Spencer's *The Shepherd's Calendar*, 1579; and Sidney's *Arcadia*, 1590) and the Accession Day Tilts, which were allegorical tournaments staged in her honour by her courtiers. (See Frances Yates, *Astraea*, 1975.)

The pastorale also had an influence on the early Italian **opera**, especially those written by Torquato Tasso (*Aminta*, 1573) and Giambattista Guarini (*The Faithful Shepherd*, 1590). It was for plays like these that Serlio designed a pastoral scene as one of the three perspective stages in his *Archittetura* (1569). Most, if not all, early operas had at least one arcadian scene. Even the proto opera, the **intermezzi** designed by Buontalenti for the wedding festival of Ferdinand de Medici in 1589, had four different pastoral scenes: a mythical garden, a mountain pasture, a forest and a "glory" which was transformed into a pastoral scene.[65] One of the favourite sources of early opera, the Orpheus myth (the hero who charms the forces of darkness with his *music*), is set in an arcadian location, and of course the heroine, Eurydice, is a shepherdess (see **opera** and Peri's *Eurydice*, 1600 and Monteverdi's *Orfeo*, 1607).

(See also, William Empson, *Some Versions of the Pastoral*, 1935.)

PATAPHYSICS

"The science of imaginary solutions (Eugene Ionesco)." An esoteric study of a highly secret society of brilliant artists and intellectuals residing mainly in Europe (but with secret branches in North America). The founding father (posthumously awarded title) was Alfred Jarry (*Ubu Roi*, 1905); the current(?) president is Eugene Ionesco (this cannot be determined with certainty as the list of officers is classified and unknown even to the membership). The founding movement in which this science was practised was **dada**; a far too respectible and

---

[65] A.M. Nagler, *Theatre Festivals of the Medici*, (New Haven: Yale Univ. Press, 1964), pp. 71-72.

coherent modern version was **absurdism** (see **Trickster**; cf. the Rhinoceros Party and Ionesco's *Rhinoceros*, 1960.)

PATHOS

(Greek: "suffering") A term used by Aristotle to identify an element of a tragedy's structure (**plot**) in the sense of "the third part (of the plot) is suffering."[66] That Aristotle ranked *pathos* with recognition (*anagnorisis*) and the turning point (*peripetia*) is a possible indication of tragedy's ritual origins in mystery cults and/or shamanism: the religious and psychological function of the tragedy (or "end") being a purgation of "suffering" through the *pathos* of the hero. (See also **ur drama**.)

PEDROLINO

A character type of the *zanni* class in the **commedia dell'arte**; a naive valet. Other versions of this character include *Pagliacchio* and *Pierrot*.

PERFORMANCE

The public display of *extra*-ordinary ability. Performance tends to create **theatre**, but it may or may not involve **drama**. When it does, however, performance stands between drama (text) and theatre (event) as a transformational catalyst.

Such a necessarily broad definition includes dance, music, and a host of other activities which might fit, that is, some which may not normally be thought of as performances (such as lectures).

PERFORMANCE ART

A **post modern** form of performance which places its emphasis on *process* rather than *product*; in which the creative **presence** of the artist is often the subject (in the sense that we witness an act of artistic creation within a context of arbitrarily

---

[66]Aristotle, *Poetics*, chapter 11, 1452b, 10-12.

chosen and structured ideas and themes). Performance art can encompass any of the following elements and attitudes:

1. an artist's interaction with various media, from the human body to video images and recordings;

2. images and sounds and the **tableau**, rather than words-in-dialogue are given priority as audience directed messages;

3. a rejection of role playing (is this possible?) and a rejection of a pre-planned structure (that is, an un-matrixed performance: see **happenings**);

4. an attempt, through the above, to create a new **dramaturgy** based on a non-causal model of human perception, cognition and creativity (e.g., association, intuition, chance or spontaneity).

PERFORMANCE DRAMATURGY

That branch of **dramaturgy** concerned with the **codes** of performance, such as vocal inflection, gesture, facial expression, movement, **business**, interpretation (of text, character etc.) and character relationships. The addition of these codes to a text is *transformational*: that is, what existed merely as a body of organized words has become a living performance.

Performance dramaturgy also includes the **mise en scene**, or staged picture, that is, the *composite* or **multi-modal communication system**. This includes all of the sights, sounds and movements of performance, from costumes to sound effects, from properties to lighting. (See also **production dramaturgy, textual dramaturgy** and **reception dramaturgy**.)

PERFORMANCE TEXT

Similar to the **prompt book** insofar as a performance text includes the codes of **performance dramaturgy**, but different in that it is not concerned with **production dramaturgy**. In other words, it includes everything brought to the text by the actor and director, but not by the designers or technicians. Consequently, we may conclude that a performance text is an *interpreted* text in preparation for performance.

Some of the plays of Tom Robertson (see *Caste*, 1867) are virtual performance texts in that they contain such detailed stage directions. Since Robertson not only wrote the play, but directed the first production for the Bancrofts at the Prince of Wales Theatre (1867), he simply wove his staging plans through the dialogue.

PERFORMANCE THEORY

A modern concern which investigates modes of **performance** cross culturally and across disciplines. The objectives of such investigations are to find and analyze similarities and differences in function--aesthetic and social--and thus in cultural expression. The attempt has been to build a body of theory which would demonstrate that all cultures share similar needs and modes of performance, but that differences provide a *text*, or key to the culture's identity. Consequently, theoretical works from disparate fields have become the texts of performance theory.

(See Erving Goffman, *The Presentation of Self in Everyday Life*, 1959; Claude Levi-Strauss, *Structural Anthropology*, 1964; Victor Turner, *Dramas, Fields and Metaphors,* 1974; James S. Hans, *The Play of the World,* 1981; Richard Scheckner, *The End of Humanism: Writings on Performance*, 1982 and *Between Theatre and Anthropology,* 1985; Michael Vanden Heuvel, *Performing Drama / Dramatizing Performance*, 1991.)

PERFORMANCE TRIAD

A term for the interactive (**synergistic**) relationship between the three principal elements of the theatrical event: performer(s), setting (or physical context), and audience. While each element is essential to **performance**, it is the interaction between the three and a text (written or otherwise) which generates meaning. In the process, dual relationships are usually formed in which two sides of the triad are given prominence while the third serves as a context. For example, a performer may interact with the stage environment and seem to be unaware of the existence of the

142

audience, but the audience remains the legitimizing context for the performer and stage.

PERIODICITY

Literally, the division of cultural history into "periods." The practice is rather new: the ancient world had no such divisions, the middle ages divided history as the Bible is divided--the period before and the period after Christ--while the Renaissance focused on the contrasts and similarities between the "ancients" and the "moderns," with the "dark ages" in between. Even the division of history into centuries is a relatively modern phenomenon, again the result of humanist accounts of "modern" history.

The trap in periodicity is that the desriptive title of a period, such as "The Romantic Age," is artificial and misleading and can be dangerously simplistic. Nevertheless, the study of history is at least in part the study of human time, and the division of such a vast body of events into convenient periods has served to make the subject more comprehensible. The most common periods in the study of art are also convenient, if they are used with caution (see **figure 13: "Periodicity"**). The point of such divisions is that they allow us to group works of art with similar stylistic and/or thematic characteristics together and to contrast this group with preceeding and succeeding groups. Thus, for example, Wolfflin's *Classic Art* contrasts the stylistic features of Renaissance and Baroque art in a very illuminating way.[67]

As a supplement to periodicity, the **synchronic / diachronic** paradigm for the analysis of any given work of art is particularly useful. Here the work is seen in the context of the art, ideology and events of its own time and this is compared to the same work seen as part of an historical tradition of such a form and/or style and/or theme--regardless of historical "period." Thus, for example, individual works depicting the man on horseback resonate meaningfully in the contexts of their own

---

[67]Heinrich Wolfflin, *Classic Art*, 2nd ed. (London: Phaidon, 1953).

time, but they also relate to all other equestrian portraits across time.

PERIPETIA

(Greek: "reversal") To Aristotle (*Poetics), peripetia,* or the sudden change in the hero's fortune (in tragedy, from good to bad; the opposite in comedy) was one of the three basic elements of **plot** (see also *pathos, anagnorosis*).[68]

PERSPECTIVE

(See **figures 10 & 11: "Scientific Single Point Perspective and the Renaissance Stage"**) Normally, this term refers to an optical relationship between a viewer and some object; often to the phenomena whereby objects *appear* to deminish in size as distance from the viewing eye is increased; and figuratively to an imagined **point of view** between subject and object.

In the Renaissance, perspective became a favourite artistic device in the creation of *illusions* of three dimensional scenes and spaces in painting and sculpture, of distant prospects in cartography, and of "perspective mindscapes" in literature and drama (see, e.g., Shakespeare's *King Lear*, Act III, sc. 6, in which Edgar pretends to describe the scene from the cliffs of Dover to his blind father).

In theatre, perspective scenery became the basis of visually spectacular **intermezzi** and **opera** in court performances. Here, the Godly Prince, seated at the focal point, not only had the most "perfect" view of the stage, he was also himself the subject of the celebratory entertainment.

In another sense of the word, one element can place the other "in perspective" through comparison (as the Gloucester plot serves the Lear plot in *King Lear*), or backgrounded elements can place foregrounded elements in perspective (as a **duet** can be emphasized in a **crowd**). Finally, an important aspect of Renaissance painting was "atmospheric" perspective: capturing the blurring effect of atmosphere between

---

[68]Aristotle, *Poetics*, chapter 11, 1452a, 20-30.

the viewer and distant elements in the painting; in drama and fiction "social perspective" places characters from different classes together in a scene.

(See Samuel Y. Edgerton, *The Renaissance Rediscovery of Linear Perspective*, 1975; Barnard Hewitt, *The Renaissance Stage: Documents of Serlio, Sabbattini and Furttenbach*, 1958; John White, *The Birth and Rebirth of Pictorial Space*, 1957.)

PIERROT

(See *Pedrolino*)

PIT

Refers to class-structured seating in an auditorium (as in "box, pit and gallery"): the pit was the lowest in price. The pit in the Elizabethan public theatre had no seating, while the pit in later commercial theatres had only benches. (Marie Wilton was one of the first to replace benches with numbered seats in the "pit" when she refurbished the Prince of Wales Theatre in the 1860's. Her reason for doing this was to attract higher paying middle class patrons.[69]) Ironically, the pit was ultimately taken over by the orchestra and the "dress circle" which were often the highest priced seats.

(See J.J. Lynch, *Box, Pit and Gallery: Stage and Society in Johnson's London*, 1953.)

PLATEA

(Latin: "place") The neutral location on the medieval stage where a scene is enacted; a necessary dramaturgical **convention** which made it possible to have several specific locations on the same stage (see **mansion staging**); in the Elizabethan public theatres the stage's neutrality made it possible for the playwright to locate an action with descriptive dialogoue alone.

In modern times, the neutral playing space has been used to suggest specific

---

[69]Oscar Brockett, *History of the Theatre*, p. 512.

locations in much the same way (see **new stagecraft**).

PLAY THEORY

Interest in the ritual origins of theatre as well as the complex relationships between theatrical events and non theatrical "play" has resulted in the serious study of play, games and rituals, their aesthetic and cultural relationships and their universal occurance. Such investigations have influenced modern notions of **performance** and even of **theatre** itself. (In fact, they have helped make a much more precise use of the language of theatre--and such dictionaries as this--necessary.) Certain fundamental questions arise in play theory: what are the differences between "play" and "game;" what are the similarities between "game" and "ritual;" how do all three relate to **theatre**?

(See Johann Huizinga, *Homo Ludens: a Study of the Play Element in Culture*, 1959; Roger Caillois, *Man, Play and Games*, 1961; Victor Turner, *Dramas, Fields and Metaphors: Symbolic Action in Human Society*, 1974; Eric Berne, *The Games People Play*, 1975; James S. Hans, *The Play of the World*, 1981.)

PLAY-WITHIN-A-PLAY

A **metatheatrical** convention which places the main event in a fresh perspective: some characters become an onstage audience watching a play, just as they in turn are being watched by us. Members of this onstage audience are then free to comment on the performance (thus becoming critics) and this provides the main audience with a double perspective.

In keeping with the Renaissance / Baroque penchant for all things theatrical, this device became one of several conventions of the day which drew attention to the life / theatre metaphor. Such scenes as the "Mousetrap" in *Hamlet* and "Pyramus and Thisbe" in *A Midsummer Night's Dream* are definitive of this whole fascination.

The aesthetics of the play-within-a-play has also intrigued modern playwrights, from Samuel Beckett to Tom Stoppard, giving rise to the provocative comment by Michael Goldman that "all the characters in drama are actors."[70]

PLOT

To Aristotle, plot was the "soul" of tragedy.[71] He referred to dramatic structure, or to the organization of the incidents (events, **french scenes**)--form, as opposed to content. Gustave Freytag, like Aristotle, focused on the dramatic content of plot for his theory (see **Freytag's Pyramid**). In his scheme, **exposition** was followed by a **rising action** and **complication** and so on to the **resolution**.

Dramatic structure is arguably the playwright's second most powerful control--the first being the choice of characters. The playwright is concerned not just with who is going to appear with whom in a given scene, but where that scene will be placed in the structure of the overall **action**. Further, the beginning of a new scene is often organically tied to the ending of the old: if one character leaves a three character scene, for example, he automatically creates a **duet**. Alternately, when all characters leave the scene, or the Act comes to an end, the playwright is faced with a decision: what happens next? Our interest in plot *per se* is therefore not so much with the *content* of units as with the links between them: what means are used to connect one unit with another? Does the connection occur in the text or in the audience? It is in this sense that we begin to appreciate the relationship between form and content. For example, the numerical sequence

1, 2, 3, 4, 5 . . . .

has a linear and indeterminate structure: we can predict the next unit, but not the final one. Whereas the sequence

1, 5, 2, 4, 3, 3, 4, 2, 5, 1

is circular and (possibly) repetitive.

---

[70]Michael Goldman, *The Actor's Freedom: Towards a New Theory of Drama* (New York: Anchor, 1975), p. 86.

[71]Aristotle, *Poetics,* chapters 7-11, 1451a--1452a.

A plot may be *causal*, in that its individual incidents are related to each other by cause and effect; it may be *chronological*, in which case time becomes the link; it may be *thematic*, meaning that each incident, although not directly related to the others, is related to, or illuminates a central idea. In any case, the form of a play reflects its content and conversely, the play's content (its **action**) will dictate its form. This means that the relationship between form and content is like that between glove and hand only if we presume that the *idea* came first. It is quite concievable that a form will suggest itself first, followed by an appropriate idea, which will then modify that form.

In addition to the connections between units, plot is concerned with the relative *proportions* of the units in terms of duration and with the character relationships within each unit. What is the significance, for example, of a three character play such as the following in which:

"A" and "B" have 35% of the play, but all at the beginning;
"A" and "C" have 10%, all at the end of the play;
"B" and "C" never meet alone and
"A" "B" and "C" have the remaining 55% in the middle of the play?

In terms of **presence** (time on stage) the characters are ranked:

"A" = 100%
"B" = 90%
"C" = 65%

In terms of dramatic function, "A" appears to be the mediator or at least a common denominator. In terms of relationships, that between "B" and "C" seems to be at issue. In terms of plot, however, the order of the scenes is most significant. Consider the climactic meeting of "A" and "C" at the end, for example, especially since a scene featuring the focal relationship ("B" and "C") never occurs.

This is a case where the form comes first. Now the content is needed to fill this form: who the characters are, what their situation is and what they want from each other.

POETICS

Aristotle's treatise on tragedy, written between 335 and 323 BCE. The *Poetics* has had a profound influence on western **dramaturgy** ever since. Subsequent theory and practice has either supported his views, modified them or rebelled against them. Many Renaissance commentators seriously misunderstood the *Poetics* and based influential prescriptive theories on their assumptions. (See, e.g., Julius Caesar Scaliger, *Poetics*, 1561; see also **unities**.)

The *Poetics* is incomplete: the manuscript is certainly corrupt at several points and obscure on others and the companion consideration of comedy is missing. As it stands, the *Poetics* is divided into three parts: first, the various forms of poetry are compared in order to distinguish between them in terms of *means, objects* (of imitation), *manner,* and *purpose*; second, tragedy is defined and the various terms in the definition are explained; third, epic poetry is considered and compared to tragedy (with the conclusion that tragedy is superior). (See various translations and commentaries, e.g., *Aristotle's Theory of Poetry and Fine Art*, S.H. Butcher, translator and editor, 3rd ed., 1902; Gerald F. Else, *Aristotle's Poetics: the Argument*, 1957.)

More generally, the word "poetics" refers to the study and theory of poetry and its **conventions** and techniques. **Dramaturgy** is the poetics of drama and theatre.

POETIC JUSTICE

One of the "rules" of neoclassic prescriptive theory, namely, the idea that in order to imitate the Real (as opposed to the mere accidents of the everyday), good characters should be rewarded and bad characters punished. This notion, that in an ideal world, the good will be triumphant, persisted through the neoclassic period and **sentimentalism**, and became the fundamental didactic conclusion of **melodrama**. Breaking this rule correspondingly became a mark of the modern drama.

POINT OF ATTACK

Faced with the complete (i.e., chronological) lives of fictional characters, or the chronological events of an existing **fable**, the playwright must decide where to begin the **action** of the play. The later the point of attack, the more **exposition** is needed to acquaint the audience with what happened previously, as in Sophocles' *Oedipus*. In such a structure, the past and its meaning necessarily becomes the focus of the action.

POINT OF VIEW (POV)

In a sense, every work of art communicates successfully by providing the viewer with "access," or a point of view, although exceptions to this can be notable for its absence. At times the POV is explicit: the viewer is told exactly how to view the work, but more often the POV is implied through a wide range of techniques.

In painting, for example, the perspective design governs the viewer's access (some religious paintings of the Renaissance added a biblical figure at the side who invited the viewer into the world of the image, as in the "St. Lucy altarpiece" by Veneziano, ca. 1445). Some sculptures are intended to be seen from one side and access is so limited, while others are meant to be seen from all sides and viewers are invited to walk around them. Most buildings not only present a specific facade to the public, they welcome visitors with a main entrance, followed by hallways leading through the interior. In music, the melodic line guides the listener through the composition. In lyric poetry the singer's voice is the personal experience being communicated; in fiction a first person narrator often supplies a point of view, or individual characters fulfill the same function.

In drama the hero and/or heroine, being the "norm" and the focus of the **action**, provide the audience with a perspective on both the action and the rest of the characters. This is particularly the case in the **commedia dell'arte** in which the unmasked lovers are the norm or "natural" from which POV the grotesques can be judged. In some plays the *raisonneur* supplies the "correct" view of the action (as in many neoclassical comedies such as Cleante in Moliere's *Tartuffe*); in other plays there is a deliberately divided point of view (as in Ibsen's *Hedda Gabler* where Hedda, Judge Braque and Lovbourg provide conflicting points of view). Samuel Beckett's major stage plays stretch and redefine the notion of POV in drama. In *Waiting for Godot* Vladimir and Estragon provide essential access into the work, but within the action, this function switches between them and even Pozzo momentarily demands that the tramps (and the audience) take his point of view. In *Endgame* the POV is split between the two main characters; in *Happy Days* Winnie totally monopolizes the POV with focused intensity; in *Krapp's Last Tape* the title character and his former selves provide us with more than one point of view at the same time. (The is the technique, incidently, used by the **play-within-the-play**, that is, where we watch another audience watching a play.)

Finally, those works which deliberately obscure or eliminate the POV do so in order to force the viewer, listener and audience to "find their own way in." In this way, the work becomes the "property" of the viewer to a greater degree than when the artist controls (or limits) access.

POLITICAL DRAMATURGY

A relatively new field of study, political dramaturgy examines the interface between life and theatre: events and activities conducted in public are subjected to a dramaturgical analysis. A political convention, for example, has many characteristics in common with the theatre. Some of these are deliberately theatrical (not just "dramatic"), others are unconsciously so. Where does life end and theatre begin? If the form is theatrical, is the content drama? If the "players" are performing according to a script (which bears a tenuous relation to reality at best), is the presentation theatre or life?

(See Art Borreca, "Political Dramaturgy, A Dramaturgs (Re) View," in *TDR*, vol. 37, No. 2, pp. 56-79; Erving Goffman, *Frame Analysis,* 1974 and *The*

Presentation of Self in Everyday Life, 1959; Elizabeth Burns, *Theatricality: a Study of Convention in the Theatre and in Social Life*, 1972.)

POOR THEATRE

A term used by the Polish director, Jerzy Grotowski (1933--) to describe a type of theatre which does not allow technology or scenery to come between the actor and the audience--the two essentials of the theatrical event. All channels of communication--aural, visual and kinetic--were to be actor generated as much as possible (we cannot discount the physical context, however plain, as part of the "message"). Thus conceived, the poor theatre was seen as a confrontation between an audience and an unencumbered actor, who interpreted a text with the tools at hand (voice, body, mind and emotion).

(See Jerzy Grotowski, *Toward a Poor Theatre*, 1968; Timothy J. Wiles, *The Theatrical Event: Modern Theories of Performance*, 1980.)

POPULAR THEATRE

A sub-category of **alternative theatre**, Popular Theatre's agenda is to use theatre and theatrical techniques to empower communities to intervene in social problems. Using improvisation and collectively created plays, groups of non professional actors engage audiences in the community with alternative solutions to social, economic, political, environmental concerns. Such projects are often commissioned, or at least requested, by social agencies within a community; at other times the company may intervene aggressively into a political or environmental crisis situation.

One of the leaders of the popular theatre movement in the United States and Canada is Augusto Boal, whose **"theatre of the oppressed"** philosophy and techniques have influenced groups with widely different constitutions and objectives. The Canadian Popular Theatre Alliance was formed in 1981, for example, to lend collective support to a variety of local groups and to facilitate nation-wide "awareness festivals," such as the "Bread and Roses" event in Edmonton in 1981.

(See Augusto Boal, *Theatre of the Oppressed*, 1979.)

POST MODERNISM

(See **modernism**) More an artistic attitude than a particular style, post modernism is a reaction against the a-political, abstract style of modernism. The term is applied quite differently, however, in the various arts. Post modern architecture, for example, is a self-conscious eclecticism in reaction to the "modernist" style of Mies van der Rohe, whose glass and steel skyscrapers look like three dimensional versions of Mondrian's abstract geometric paintings. Consequently, few, if any critics have been willing to define the term.

Post modern theatre and **performance art** are similar in that they do not limit works to any one medium, but instead deliberately mix the literary, visual and performing arts. At the same time, post modern theatre shifts away from text centred drama and toward *process*, inviting the audience into a collaborative process of creation. Post modern theatre joins with post structural theory in attempting a non-representational (or non-mimetic) theatre in which meaning is discovered "between signs and sign systems," not exclusively in the signs themselves.

(See Bonnie Maranca, *The Theatre of Images*, 1977 and the *Performing Arts Journal*; Kate Davy, *Richard Foreman and the Ontological-Hysteric Theatre*, 1981; Michael Vanden Heuvel, *Performing Drama / Dramatizing Performance*. 1991.)

POST STRUCTURALISM

(See **structuralism, deconstruction**) As applied to drama and theatre, a post-structuralist analysis assumes that every sign produced, from the word on the page to the utterance and gesture on the stage are mere approximations of ideas which belonged to others at the time of their inception. "To be or not to be" *approximated* an idea/image/feeling in Shakespeare's mind when he wrote it; the words approximated a quite different idea/image/feeling in Burbage when he spoke them (see the quotation from Samuel Beckett under **absurdism**). What counts are the ideas produced by these signs in the minds of individuals in the audience--each being different. Words on the page and actions on the stage are mere potential as meaningful signs. Such a critical stance therefore foregrounds that branch of **dramaturgy** concerned with **reception**. Post structuralism does not negate the value of structuralist analysis, but insists that in terms of *communication* it does not go far enough. (See Jacques Derrida, *Writing and Difference*, 1978.)

PRAGMATICS

The practical, as opposed to the theoretical; that branch of **semiotics** concerned with **signs**, those who produce them, and those who receive them. In the theatre, playwrights, directors and designers are all producers of signs and as such very interested in those who receive them (the audience), but it is actors who are the main pragmatic artists of the theatre. The actor in performance is in fact engaged in a cybernetic **feedback loop**, adjusting his work as he gauges response. (See **semantics, syntactics**.)

PRESENCE

The defining condition of **theatre** is the living presence of the actor(s) and audience and their relationship. It is actors' living interpretation of roles for each . performance--in a context of other living presences--that makes it unique and the production "new" each time it is performed.

Stemming from this condition is a dramaturgical fact all too often overlooked during the *reading* of a text: a character may appear on stage from a moment to extended periods of time *without speaking*. In such cases, however, his *presence* is a significant (visual) component of the total stage picture, and his presence therefore influences the action of the scene and the audience's perception of it. On the other hand, a reader will easily forget that character's presence. Consequently, when compiling dramaturgical data for analysis, the presence of each character, especially in terms relative to other characters and to **speech**, must be estimated and included.

PRESENTATIONAL THEATRE

A style of performance presented directly to the audience. Both presentational and **representational theatre** are terms which describe the aesthetic relationship of the performance to the audience, but it should be emphasized that both styles are artificial. Presentational theatre attempts to maintain an illusion of "present actuality" (which creates an aesthetic paradox of presence vs. identity), whereas representational theatre maintains an illusion of *another* actuality (which creates an aesthetic paradox of presence vs. time and space).

Many plays and productions mix the two styles and this practice implies that a **convention** is established only to be broken and re-established in a new form. When this occurs, the presentational style tends to condition the illusion of the representational portions of the performance, creating a **metatheatrical** tension. Such a phenomenon is by no means modern: the Greek theatre created such a tension between the characters, chorus and audience; many medieval **mystery** and Elizabethan plays mixed the two styles when a greater stage/audience intimacy was desired; early melodrama used the technique to underscore its moral points and so on. (Note that Heinrich Wofflin's *Classic Art*, 1953, uses similar criteria in his comparison of classic and romantic painting.)

PRIVATE THEATRE

A term used to differentiate between completely enclosed Elizabethan theatres such as Burbage's Blackfriars and the "public playhouse" with its open courtyard. A play written specifically for a private theatre had to take the physical characteristics of the venue into consideration.

PRODUCER

The producer of a play or other theatrical event is the one responsible for initiating the project, for contractual arrangements (e.g., bringing the production team together), acquiring rehearsal and performance spaces, and at least managing the budget. To this extent, the producer serves the production and its team. To the extent that the producer controls the budget, he tends to control the production.

In England, the tradition has been to call the stage director a "producer," with the above functions being the responsibility of a manager. This is a hold-over from the days when actor-managers essentially fulfilled both functions, while the stage manager conducted rehearsals.

PRODUCTION DRAMATURGY

(See **dramaturgy**) Production dramaturgy refers to elements of theatrical production, from theatre architecture to lighting equipment, all of which condition **reception** of a performance. The size, shape and stage equipment of theatres, the decorations and amenities of the **lobby**, the seating arrangements of the auditorium, even the location of the theatre in the city--affect both the production and the appreciation of it. Consider, for example, two productions of *A Midsummer Night's Dream*, one in an intimate theatre with severely limited technical capabilities and another in a large, sumptuous theatre with the latest in lighting, sound and design technology; the first with a modest budget and the second with relatively unlimited resources. Aside from the obvious fact that performances of each would be affected by its production circumstances, audiences would receive entirely different impressions of them. (See **performance** and **reception dramaturgy**.)

PROLOGOS

(Greek: "to speak before") In the classical Greek theatre, the prologue was given before the entrance of the chorus. The function of this speech at this point was usually to set the mood of the play and to set its **action** in context.

Later, prologues were simple dramaturgical devices to introduce the characters or the issues of a play. In the Restoration and through the 19th century, a prologue was simply a speech given by an actor to introduce the play to the audience, usually on behalf of the playwright.

To the extent that a prologue discusses the action, its characters and issues, it has dramaturgical significance in that it conditions the audience's expectations.

PROMPT

Usually a line or a cue given to an actor during rehearsals and even performances. In former times, when rehearsals were few and the time given to memorize a text was short, such prompts were a major feature of a performance, with the prompter's box protruding above the stage floor down centre. These circumstances obviously had a significant effect on the **performance dramaturgy** of the production. For example, it usually meant that actors never strayed far from a position in front of the prompter's box, which restricted blocking and limited audience appreciation for the physical potential of the text. Consequently, such elements of **production dramaturgy** must be given consideration in any historical analysis of performances.

PROMPT BOOK

Originally a "prompter's book," meaning that it was used simply to **prompt** actors during performances. Such a book might include marked entrances and exits as well as lines, but little more.

More recently, the prompt book became the work book and property of the Stage Manager, who noted blocking and business, sound and light cues, set changes and entrances and exits.

Historically, the appearance of the (modern) prompt book signalled major changes in play production: blocking had become more complex and meaningful, controllable electric lighting produced multiple light cues and so on. (See **performance text**, *modellbuch.*).

PROPERTIES

From the beginning, it would appear, dramatic texts have drawn attention to objects on the stage:

> OEDIPUS: What is the meaning of this supplication,
> These *branches and garlands* . . . .[72]

but such embedded references barely hint at the complex layers of meaning such objects can suggest during a performance. Properties make a visual statement and have a certain "durability" for an audience which is denied a reader, resulting in a theatrical meaning which transcends the written words. What do the "branches and garlands" above actually look like? Why does Oedipus feel they are worth mentioning? What do they mean to the suppliants, to Oedipus and to the Athenian audience? It what way are they visual codes for the death and sterility of the plague? As these questions imply, properties constitute an important dramaturgical **code system**.

When a prop is both mentioned in dialogue and handled by a character, its meaning is energized through a constellation of relationships. In the following instance, the mental vision of a prop leads to an action and the appearance of the actual prop:

> Is this a dagger which I see before me,
> The handle toward my hand? Come, let me clutch thee.
> I have thee not, and yet I see thee still.
> Art thou not, fatal vision, sensible
> To feeling as to sight? or art thou but
> A dagger of the mind, a false creation,
> Proceeding from the heat-oppressed brain?
> I see thee yet, in form as palpable
> As this which now I draw.
> *Macbeth*: II,1

"As palpable / As this which now I draw" is a line containing a visual/kinetic code and a reference to a prop which is an **index** of the dagger which killed Duncan.

In Ibsen's *Hedda Gabler*, a pistol is handled by Hedda at the beginning of Act

---

[72]Sophocles, *King Oedipus*, trans. E.F. Watling (Harmondsworth, Middlesex: Penguin, 1947), p. 25, l. 2-3.

II. This pistol is one of a set of duelling pistols which belonged to her father (now dead). She shoots the pistol playfully at Judge Brack, who represents the establishment, and it is the same pistol she kills herself with at the end. This pistol, at this moment in the play, consequently defines character relationships while tying an aristocratic past to a tragic future.

There are also historical and sociological implications to the relationships established by properties. In each age, objects are a function of man's connection to the physical and social world. For example, it is not simply coincidental that **realism, naturalism** and the proliferation of properties on stage occurred with the rise of the middle class to economic power and middle class drama to a position of major influence. Aside from other considerations, *things* were important signs of the materialism of the class and its upward mobility and thus of the relative status of characters.

Dramaturgically, properties and how they are used by characters are another means the playwright has to reveal character and **subtext**. At the same time a prop can gain symbolic density through repeated appearances in different contexts in the play and such appearances help structure the **action**. In addition to Hedda's duelling pistols, for example, the manuscript of Lovbourg's new book appears (or is mentioned) several times during the play. To Lovbourg himself it is a vindication of his life, to Tesman it represents an embarrassing contrast to his own pedantic research, to Thea it represents a "child" (a product of her creative assistance to Lovbourg's work), and to Hedda it represents her own failure to have such a creative influence.

PROSCENIUM ARCH

(See **figures 10 & 11**) An arch which forms a "picture frame" around the front of the stage, thus setting the characters and action at an **aesthetic distance** from the audience. This means that the arch separates the here and now of the audience from the *illusion* of other times and places.

The proscenium arch was a necessary device for the creation of **perspective scenery** in the Italian Renaissance (and it helped hide stage machinery). A proscenium necessitates a frontal view of the stage and creates problematic sight lines: the auditorium cannot be significantly wider than the arch or those seated at the extremes will see only part of the stage, which means, in turn, that the blocking of the actors is limited.

The first (known) use of a permanent proscenium was built by Buontalenti in the Uffizi palace in Florence in 1586 (for the Medici; see **opera**). The oldest surviving proscenium is in the Teatro Farnese, in Parma, built in 1618.

PROTAGONIST

(Greek: "first contestant") The chief agent of a play's **action** and usually its initiator; opposed by the **antagonist**. (See also **tritagonist**.)

PULCINELLA

A character of the *zanni* class in the **commedia dell'arte**. Pulcinella was a physically grotesque, often brutish character of low intelligence. However, this description also reflects contemporary social stereotyping: common people were thought to be something less than fully human (see **figure 9**). The English "Punch" had similar characteristics and was probably derived from the commedia.

Q

QUARTET

The quartet appears to be the largest, practical, relational unit: four people on stage together can function as a group of individuals and be comprehended by an audience, whereas five characters become a "crowd" which tends to be variously subdivided (e.g., into a **duet** and a **trio**), if not by the playwright and director, then by the audience.

The playwright has a difficult juggling act to perform: keeping four characters fully involved in a scene is not a simple task. One of the most successful attempts in modern drama is *Who's Afraid of Virginia Woolf?* by Edward Albee. Albee's solution to the dramaturgy of the four character play is to divide them into two contrasting pairs: young vs. middle aged, male vs. female and hosts vs. guests. These **given circumstances** are emphasized in the early quartet scenes, with the lines separating the two couples clearly marked as the characters become acquainted. Later, and because of this preparation, Albee is able to divide the quartet into a variety of smaller units, only bringing them all together for climactic confrontations.

The number of *possible* combinations offered by a four character play is surprising. By merely adding one character to a trio, the number of combinations increases from eight to 16:

```
0.....................................................................(empty stage)
(A), (B), (C), (D)...................................................(as solos)
A+B, A+C, A+D / B+C, B+D / C+D................................(as duets)
A+B+C, A+B+D, A+C+D / B+C+D...............................(as trios)
A+B+C+D...........................................................(as a quartet)
```

Albee makes use of 12 of these possibilities in a total of 37 **french scenes**. He includes three solos, 22 duets, 27 trios and seven quartets. Significantly, Martha and Honey never appear alone together, nor do Honey and Nick. The important question is why not? On the other hand, all possible trio combinations are used. Again, the question is why? These are the playwright's dramaturgical choices; an analysis of the text must take them into account.

QUARTO

In early (English) printing practices, the division of a standard sheet of paper into four equal parts, which then became the dimension of a printed book (approximately 7" X 9"). The majority of Shakespeare's plays were printed in quarto form before they appeared in a **folio** edition (1623).

QUEM QUAERITIS

(Latin: "whom do you seek . . . .") Traditionally cited as the first documented **liturgical drama** (an extended **trope**),[73] and it includes directions for production--making it one of the first **performance texts**. It was found in the *Regularis Concordia*, compiled by the Bishop of Winchester cathedral around 975 AD. It is an Easter trope and it involves the three Marys coming to the empty tomb in search of Christ.

There are several significant features in this playlet, including role playing, men portraying female characters, the scene directions, embedded references to **properties**, the use of a dramatic text in the midst of the **ritual** of the **Mass**. Since the lines were sung (the music exists[74]), the *Quem Quaeritis* is also a miniature **opera**.

(See Mary Marshall, "Aesthetic Values of the Liturgical Drama," in *Medieval*

---

[73]Oscar Brockett, *History of the Theatre*, p. 109.

[74]*Quem Quaeritis*, St. Gall MS: 484, Ex. 56 (1), p. 111.

English Drama, 1975; O.B. Hardison, *Christian Rite and Christian Drama in the Middle Ages*, 1965.)

R

RAISONNEUR

(French: "reasoner") From French **neoclassicism**, which gave priority to reason over emotion. The *raisonneur* is the character in a play who functions as the touchstone of reason in an **action** which involves a conflict between duty and passion (in tragedy) or between "natural" and "unnatural" behaviour (in comedy). The role of the *raisonneur* was at times combined with that of the *confidante* (or "side kick"). The *raisonneur* was (is) also often used as a vehicle for the playwright's views.

REALISM

(See **figure 4: "realism"**) A theatrical *style*, which attempts to create an illusion of actuality through the **code systems** of **setting, properties, costumes,** lighting and acting (speech, gesture and movement). Realism depends on a strict **convention** which clearly separates the world of the audience from the world of the stage (facilitated by, but not limited to, the use of the **proscenium arch**). Realism is by no means limited to the theatre, as analogous movements occurred in European painting and literature during the 19th century. Realism as a style of presentation should be distinguished from **naturalism** as a theory of human behaviour.

(See Eric Auerbach, *Mimesis, Representations of Reality in Western Literature*, 1953; J.L. Styan, *Modern Drama in Theory and Practice*, vol 1, 1981)

RECEPTION THEORY

When a playwright's **code systems** are interpreted and augmented by a director and actors for performance, an audience receives and *decodes* these systems according to understood **conventions**. Other considerations which influence understanding, however, include audience demographics and social context: age, gender, occupation, education and race; social norms, ideology, current events.

Reception theory is that branch of **dramaturgy** which concerns itself with how audience's gain "meaning" (both collective and individual) from theatrical events. Reception theory is also a branch of **semiotics**, and has recently been the subject of much speculation and research by theatre semioticians such as Marco De Marinis, Umberto Eco and Patrice Pavis. (See Susan Bennett, *Theatre Audiences: a Theory of Production and Reception,* 1990).

The major problem with theatrical reception research is the difficulty in analyzing such a complex **multi-modal communication system** which is not only *ephemeral*, it is also interpreted by audiences made up of distinct individuals. The trap is believing that the "meaning" produced is free of ambiguity and that the performance is received uniformly.

(See also, Robert C. Holub, *Reception Theory: a Critical Introduction*, 1984; Christopher Butler, *Interpretation, Deconstruction and Ideology*, 1984.)

RECITATIVE

Dramatic dialogue set to music; operatic speech; musical notation intended to imitate the inflections of natural speech; a musical vehicle which is open and flexible enough to carry the dramatic action forward between **arias**. Historically, the invention of recitative in the late 16th century by artists of the Florentine humanist *camarata*, such as Peri, was the breakthrough required in the development of **opera**.

(See Donald J. Grout, *A Short History of Opera*, 1977; Robert Donnington, *The Rise of Opera*, 1981.)

RECOGNITION

(See *anagnorosis)*

REDUNDANCY

A term from communications theory referring to the built-in redundancy of all message systems: technically, the broadcast of more "message" than is necessary for comprehension, through repetition, embellishment and qualification. (See Jeremy Campbell, *Grammatical Man: Information, Entropy, Language and Life*, 1982).

In the theatrical event, which is a **"multi-modal communication system,"** it is redundancy which makes the complexity of the system coherent, for the more complex the system, the more likely it is that one of its channels will malfunction, or simply be missed. Thus, for example, words, vocal inflection, facial expression, gesture and movement are all driven by the same **objective** and carry the same subtextual message. Voice, movement, setting and costume can reinforce the mood of a scene from their respective aural, visual and kinetic channels. On the other hand, channels differ in strength and "decay time:" movement is stronger than speech, settings last longer than sounds. Consequently, there is a danger that supportive redundancy can become counter-productive "static."

RELACOM

Robert Cohen's term for "relationship communication" in acting theory and practice. When we interact socially (and theatrically), we invoke *relationships*--often unconsciously--as the underlying basis by which others are to interpret the content of our messages. We do this through vocal inflection and volume, facial expression, body language and even the words themselves--they are, after all, chosen by us. For example, I can attempt to invoke a master/slave relationship with you by shouting, sneering, pointing and threatening. (See Robert Cohen, *Acting Power*, 1978.)

RELATIVE MOTION

Just as some characters are more talkative than others, some are more active. Motion on stage (**blocking**) is generally created by director/actor experimentation and agreement in rehearsal, but much of it can be controlled by the playwright through kinetic **codes** in the dialogue. In *Riders to the Sea*, for example, Synge has deliberately made the younger daughter, Nora, by far the most active character on stage, thus highlighting not only her youth, but also Cathleen's relative maturity and authority by contrast. In this way Nora communicates kinetically against a general background of stillness: she is a **sign** of vitality in a community preoccupied with death.

For the actor, **presence, speech** and relative motion are the visual, aural and kinetic channels of communication.

REPERTOIRE

(French: "stock list; repertory") (a) An actor's stock roles and/or audition pieces which are more or less ready for performance; (b) a company's stock of repeated plays; (c) plays performed *in repertory* are performed alternately. The repertory system presupposes a permanent theatre company and has usually required subsidy or patronage (such as the National Theatre in England and the *Comedie Francaise* in France).

REPRESENTATIONAL THEATRE

(See **presentational theatre**)

RESOLUTION

(See **denouement**)

RESTORATION DRAMA

A brief, but vital sub period in the history of English drama, theatre and dramatic criticism between 1660 (the "restoration" of Charles II) and 1688 (his death), although works in the "restoration style" were being written and produced through the end of the century (e.g., Congreve's *The Way of the World*, 1700). From the perspective of this later date, however, restoration drama becomes a transition between **neoclassicism**, which functioned as a vehicle for absolutism, and **sentimentalism**, which responded to an ascendant middle class ideology.

Restoration drama brought back to England a version of French neoclassicism, tempered by the social mores and fashions of the French court at Versailles (where Charles and his entourage were in exile). **Heroic tragedy** was the English version of the neoclassic tragedy of Corneille and Racine in which themes such as love vs. honour were set in heroic couplets (see Dryden's *Indian Queen*, 1664). The English attitude toward this artificial style, however, was made obvious by the successful parody by the Duke of Buckingham (George Villiers) in *The Rehearsal*, 1671. More importantly, it was the restoration comedy of wit and manners which became a brilliantly distinctive and decadent style--"decadent" in that it expressed the mores and fashions of a dying class, the "swan songs" of aristocratic hegemony in England. It was a style soon replaced by the sentimental comedies and melodramas of the middle class.

(See Thomas J. Fugimura, *The Restoration Comedy of Wit*, 1952; John Russell Brown and Bernard Harris, eds., *Restoration Theatre*, 1965; John Loftis, *Restoration Drama: Modern Essays in Criticism*, 1966; J.L. Styan, *Restoration Comedy in Performance*, 1986; Simon Callow, *Acting in Restoration Comedy*, 1991. See also essays by Dryden, Congreve, Rhymer and Collier.)

REVELS

Strictly speaking, the revels were the court dances conducted at special state occasions, especially after a **masque** and before a banquet. The dancers included the masquers and the court ladies in the audience.

The position of "Master of the Revels" was a royal patronage position dating from the time of Elizabeth and revived by Queen Victoria, who awarded it to Charles Keene in 1848. The position evolved from that of a ceremonial functionary at state banquets to one of some control of licences and censorship in the Victorian theatre.

REVENGE PLAY

Not a true **genre**; the term refers to a frequent theme in Elizabethan and Jacobean tragedy (e.g., *The Revenger's Tragedy, The Spanish Tragedy, Hamlet, Antonio's Revenge*) which was obviously a favourite subject of the audience. While the archetype of the theme was Greek (e.g., the *Orestia*), the model tended to be Senecan: the Elizabethan and especially the Jacobean form was often steeped in bizarre violence and focused on political feuds created by corrupt courts.

REVIEW

Not true dramatic criticism, but a brief (often critical) account of the opening of a play (or film or gallery) for a newspaper audience. Reviews tend to be superficial and written in haste, but often wield much power over the financial success of a production. On the other hand, many reviews in major papers and magazines, from the days of the *Spectator* (18th century), through those of G.B. Shaw to the present day, have been thoughtfully written by journalists with wide experience (often specific expertise), and are perceptive guides to quality acting, directing and playwrighting.

REVUE

(See **figure 12**) In England during the first quarter of this century, a revue was similar to most music hall entertainments such as the variety and **vaudeville**, with a loosely structured string of satirical sketches, songs and dances.

In the U.S., however, the revue, under the leadership of Tony Pastor, Florence Ziegfeld and George. M. Cohen, became a major force in musical theatre, leading eventually to **musical comedy**. The main difference between the American revue and vaudeville was the attempt to give the show coherence through themes and/or the works of popular song writers. The careers of some of America's major composers and writers gained prominence through revues, "scandals" and "follies:" George and Ira Gershwin, Cole Porter, Irving Berlin and Lorenz Hart, for example.

(See G. Bordman, *American Musical Revue: from The Passing Show to Sugar Babies*, 1985.)

RHETORIC

Traditionally, rhetoric has been limited to the art of effective, that is, persuasive speaking and writing. Oratory was a much respected art in ancient Greece, with Pericles one of the most renowned speakers and the Sophists its strongest advocates and teachers. Through medieval theologians and later Italian humanists, rhetoric became the foundation of education throughout Europe.

In the "rebirth of classical learning" which characterized Renaissance art and scholarship, rhetoric and the rules governing its practice became a major preoccupation with the humanists. These neoplatonic scholars, in the service of wealthy merchant princes such as the Medicis, extended the scope of rhetoric to include all of the "arts of persuasion," (i.e., communication) such as painting, sculpture, music, dance and theatre. In the process, criteria for a vocabulary of rhetorical forms applicable by analogy to all of the arts were developed. Such concepts as *inventio* (artistic invention), *dispositio* (structural arrangement), *ethopoea* (nobility of character) and *expressio* (emotional expression/underlying passion) were prescribed to insure that a work of art effectively mirrored the laws of divine proportion and harmony .

The philosophical purpose of such rhetorical forms was to bridge the gap between this world of phenomena and the ideal world of essences, between the mundane and the sublime. The ideological purpose, by extension, was to demonstrate the conviction that the hierarchy of Being was both true and permanent and that the patron (often the explicit subject) was divinely ordained to rule (hence: "Godly Prince"). (See **figure 9: "Neoplatonism and the Great Chain of Being"**.)

When applied to a synthesis of the arts, as in the development of **opera**, the rules of rhetoric were thought to accomplish the same ends even more effectively. Divine proportion and harmony, equally the criteria of words, music and visual spectacle, were more assured and their persuasive impact more guaranteed by the arts in combination (**synergy**). Opera (including the architectual space of its performance) thus became the most characteristic form of **baroque** absolutism.

(See Paul Oscar Kristeller, *Renaissance Thought and its Sources,* 1979; Michael Baxandall, *Giotto and the Orators: Humanist Observers of Painting and the Discovery of Pictorial Composition 1350-1450,* 1971.)

RHYTHM

Rhythm is the soul of all artistic expression. The following are all attempts to characterize/define what rhythm is and how it functions:

The life line between art and audience.
"The functioning of a structure." (Kenneth Burke)
"It don't mean a thing, if it ain't got that swing." (Duke Ellington)
The catalyst between form and content.
"Orderly, perceptible changes." (Richard Boleslavsky)
"Alternating pulses of storm and calm." (Raymond Bayer)
"Interdependent tension and release." (Susan K. Langer)

Since a theatrical event is a **multi-modal communication system**, it is not only structured by the specific rhythms of individual modes (e.g., words, music, movements, settings) and the structure of the work itself, it is characterized by the *interactions* of these rhythms--some of long, others of shorter duration. Such a complex interweaving of different rhythms obviously needs orchestration to achieve a unified, or at least a desired, effect.

Rhythm must be clearly distinguished from *tempo* or *pace*: rhythm is structure through repetition; tempo is the speed of that structure. A speech, for example, can be spoken at different tempos, but have the same rhythm. (See Kathleen George, *Rhythm in Drama,* 1980.)

RISING ACTION

This refers to the build in tension up to the **climax** of the play; in terms of **Freytag's Pyramid**, the section of rising action lies between the introduction (**exposition**) and the climax. (See **complication**.)

RITUAL

A pattern of activity of some consequence to an individual and/or community which is repeated with regularity (i.e., a ritual is not a one time only activity). It is important to differentiate between *play* (or game), *habit, ritual* and *theatre*: the difference lies in how the activity is perceived by those involved. Play is inconsequential in that it is self contained, voluntary, and has no utility beyond itself (a hockey game is play; the Stanley Cup is a ritual); a habit tends to be unconsciously and compulsively repeated (smoking is a habit; smoking as part of an execution is a ritual); a ritual is perceived as having some individual or communal benefit and thus significance (a spontaneous pot luck dinner is trivial; an annual box social is a ritual); theatre occurs when the activity is separated from the observers by **aesthetic distance** (to the stage manager it is a job; to the audience it is art).

Spectator games can, depending on audience perception, fall on that line separating game from theatre; theatre, in turn, can be perceived as ritual if those involved perceive it so (the **Mass** can be seen as *either* ritual or theatre, but never both at the same time). In fact, theatre's roots, forms and functions are so close to ritual that the difference is difficult to define--it becomes a matter of degrees of seriousness or consequence. Generally, however, theatre is **displaced** ritual. Those forms of theatre intended for pure entertainment and which require the most passive involvement are those displaced furthest from ritual. (See **play theory.**)

See Richard Scheckner and Mady Schuman, eds., *Ritual, Play and Performance*, 1976; Victor Turner, *From Ritual to Theatre*, 1982.)

ROMANCE

(See **figure 1: "The Ur Drama"**) In Northrop Frye's paradigm, romance occurs within the idealized landscape of an apocalyptic world.[75] It is the polar

---

[75]Frye, *Anatomy of Criticism*, Third Essay, "Archetypal Criticism: Theory of Myths."

opposite of irony and satire, which describes a demonic world. In the natural cycle, romance falls within the boundaries of afternoon or summer, whereas irony occurs within night or winter. Romances are characterized by adventure in which the hero (typically) or heroine is engaged in a quest. The dramatic equivalent of the romance is **melodrama**, whereas irony and satire find their dramatic expression in farce and tragicomedy.

(See M.H. Abrams, *The Mirror and the Lamp*, 1953; Northrop Frye, *The Secular Scripture: a Study of the Structure of Romance*, 1978.)

ROMANESQUE

"In the Roman style:" the romanesque designates a style of medieval church architecture and analogously, all of the arts between approximately 900 and 1100 AD. Romanesque abbey cathedrals along the various pilgrimage routes were built like fortresses, with thick walls, rounded arches and rather plain exteriors. The romanesque style reflected an ecclesiastical austerity: a doctrine based on earthly suffering, the terrors of damnation and the mystery of salvation. Romanesque drama and theatre was liturgical (see **trope**).

ROMANTICISM

Both a general movement in the arts (ca. 1775-1875) and a fundamental attitude toward the relationships between the individual and society, between the artist and nature and between the arts themselves. Perhaps better described as a "romantic spirit" than a movement, romanticism was first evident in literature and literary theory,[76] but was soon echoed in painting and music and other aspects of European and (later) American culture. Romantic philosophy, especially in Germany and France, begins with Kant, whose rationalist *critiques* contain the seeds of personalized, *feeling based* aesthetics, and includes such diverse writers as Rousseau,

---

[76]M.H. Abrams, *The Mirror and the Lamp: Romantic Theory and the Critical Tradition* (New York: W.W. Norton, 1953).

Burke, Nietzsche and Schopenhauer. By 1800 the "romantic/classic" debate permeated every aspect of social and artistic discourse.

What began as a rebellion against **neoclassicism** and the restrictions of the establishment in the Age of Enlightenment, soon became a programme which redefined the fundamental relationships in western culture: man, God (nature), society and art. Works of art were no longer thought of merely as "nature to advantage dressed,"[77] or as a "mirror" of nature, but as products of personal expression and "natural" genius. Through the Renaissance and Baroque periods, genius had been defined in terms of quality and technical virtuosity: a "genius" was a master craftsman. Now, genius was defined in terms of a unique personality, a manifestation of creative nature not to be restricted by artificial rules and limits. The artist's function was no longer to copy nature, but to *respond* to nature subjectively. Since the artist's vision was both unique and passionate, it was likely to be misunderstood by society. The result, an alienated artist and a marginalized art--the birth of the **avant garde**.

While the primary source of inspiration for the romantic artist was the unexplored *self*, other sources included nature, the poor, liberty and nationalism, the mysterious, the exotic and ancient, and the heroic rebel. Artistic form became a ground for experimentation, and the "total art work" (Wagner's ***gesamkunstwerk***), with music as the catalyst, a new ideal.

A strong theme of melancholy can be found in most late romantic art, however, as artists began to confront an inevitable dilemma predicted by Kant: lofty personal ideals were unattainable from within an imperfect world and a corrupt society. Suicide, lovers' death pacts and other forms of self destruction became obsessions. Great hope at the beginning of a work became utter despair by its end (cf. Beethoven's 5th symphony, Coleridge's *Kubla Khan*, the paintings of Caspar David Friedrich, Wagner's *Tristan und Isolde*, Goethe's *Faust*).

---

[77]Alexander Pope, *Essay on Criticism*, II, 297.

Romanticism in drama and theatre tended toward the spectacular (and unstageable), or to the highly subjective (and incomprehensible). In between lay romantic (or "grand") opera at one extreme of music theatre and melodrama at the other. The one tended to be swan songs of a dying aristocracy, the other morally reassuring entertainment for an ascendant middle class.

(See F. Schiller, *Maria Stuart*, 1800; P.B. Shelley, *The Cenci*, 1819; V. Hugo, *Hernani*, 1830; G. Meyerbeer, *Robert the Devil* (grand opera), 1831; E. Rostand, *Cyrano de Bergerac*, 1898.)

Romanticism influenced all forms of avant garde theatre, however, from the subjective "dream plays" of August Strindberg to the screams of alienation of the expressionists, from the arcane symbolists to the bizarre surrealists.

(See M.H. Abrams, *The Mirror and the Lamp: Romantic Theory and the Critical Tradition*, 1953; Arnold Hauser, *The Social History of Art*, 1956; Wylie Sypher, *From Rococo to Cubism in Art and Literature,* 1960; Marvin Carlson, *The French Stage in the 19th Century*, 1972, and *The German Stage in the 19th Century*, 1972; Hugh Honour, *Romanticism*, 1979; Frederick Brown, *Theatre and Revolution*, 1980; Francis Claudon, *The Concise Encyclopedia of Romanticism*, 1986.)

S

SAINTS' PLAY

A medieval **liturgical drama**, developed in the Romanesque abbey schools (probably as didactic lessons), concerned with the life of a saint, martyr or prophet.

SATYR PLAY

Generically the ancestor of **farce**, the ancient Greek satyr play was a licentious, anarchic parody of myth, legend, historical personages and even of the tragedies they followed in the dramatic festivals of Athens. Only one complete satyr play has survived, Euripides' *Cyclops*, and most of Sophocles' *Trackers*. (See **figure 1: 'The Ur Drama."**)

Satyrs, who were the companions of Dionysus, led by the drunken Silenus, possibly share the **trickster** archetype: they were half human, pleasure loving creatures of gross appetites and amoral drives.

(See E.T. Kirby, *Ur Drama: the Origins of Theatre*, 1975; general studies of Greek tragedy and comedy.)

SCENARIO

The dramaturgical equivalent of the precis; a summary of a plot; such a summary used in the **commedia dell'arte** as a guide to an improvised performance; a more detailed script for a motion picture.

The scenario is the quintessential *blueprint* for performance in that it throws the focus on the actor/audience relationship. In such a case, the full text only appears after the performance, as a record.

SCENE A FAIRE

(See **obligatory scene**)

SCENE

(From Greek, *skene*: "hut," or "place".) (Colloquially) a location in which dramatic characters in situations appear (see **setting**); a dramaturgical unit defined by entrances and exits (see **french scene**) or by **systemic changes.**

In Kenneth Burke's system, the "scene" is one of five elements in all literary texts (the "pentad") which includes: the "act" (what happened), the "scene" (where it occurred), the "agent" (who did it), the "agency" (how it was done) and the "purpose" (why it was done).[78] (For the actor, "agency" and "purpose" are **tactics** and **objectives.**)

SCENE DIRECTIONS

(See **stage directions**) Generally, scene directions include anything written in the text concerning characters, situation and setting which is *not* dialogue. Scene directions are often useful as aids to a reader's comprehension of *intended* stage representation, but since they are not organic, they may or may not be relevant to the *actual* staging. Such directions are often embellished after a first production for the published version and some are not even written by the playwright. Consequently, all scene directions should be treated with caution. On the other hand, a line of dialogue such as "come here and sit beside me on the couch" must affect bother the setting (the couch) and the blocking. A scene direction to the same effect can be ignored by actors, director and designer.

---

[78]Kenneth Burke, *A Rhetoric of Motives*, 2nd ed. (New York: Scribners, 1969), p. 27.

Historically, scene directions became a function of the development of **realism** and the emergence of the stage director. The plays of Tom Robertson (1829-71), which were at the forefront of Victorian realism, contain a high proportion of scene directions--nearly one third of the printed lines of *Caste*, for example, are scene directions. Since Robertson directed his own plays, these scene directions amount to a **performance text**. They contain notes on blocking, setting, props, character analysis and actor delivery. Similarly, the plays of George Bernard Shaw contain copious scene directions--in addition to lengthy prefaces--both indications of his profound understanding of the **ambiguity** and thus possible misinterpretation of language on the stage.

More recently, some playwrights have reverted to the earlier practice (e.g., Elizabethan) of **embedding** directions in the dialogue as a mechanism of control over performance. The opposite strategy has also been adopted by some modern playwrights: by leaving most directions out all together, the ambiguity is increased, giving the actors and director more interpretive freedom.

SEMANTICS

In **semiotics**, the meanings of words: a word is a *signifier*, its meaning is the *signified*, and together they constitute a **sign**. (See also **syntactics, pragmatics**.)

SEMIOTICS

The study of **signs** and sign systems, originally applying to linguistics, now embracing all forms of communication. A sign is a **code** made up of a relationship between a *signifier* and a *signified*: e.g., the letters **B, A, L, L** (when written in this configuration) signify a spherical object which bounces (see also **icon, index, symbol**). Theatre semiotics is concerned with all meaning producing **code systems** in the theatre, from text to auditoriums, and how they are interpreted (decoded) by audiences.

(See Umberto Eco, *A Theory of Semiotics*, 1976; Terrence Hawkes,

Structuralism and Semiotics, 1977; Kier Elam, *The Semiotics of Theatre and Drama,* 1980; Patrice Pavis, *Problems of a Semiotics of Gesture,* 1980; Erika Fisher-Lichte, *The Semiotics of Theatre,* 1983; trans. 1992; Elaine Aston and George Savona, *Theatre as Sign System: a Semiotics of Text and Performance,* 1992.)

SENICAN

A tragedy in the style of Seneca (4 BCE-65 AD), who was much admired in the Renaissance (especially among the Elizabethans). The style included some or all of the following characteristics:

1. Sensationalism and the (evil) extremes of human behaviour (e.g., incest, infanticide), violence and horror;

2. the **revenge** theme, especially the revenge of a child for the murder of a parent (e.g., *The Spanish Tragedy, Hamlet*); intrigue;

3. ghosts (e.g., of a wronged person, such as Hamlet's father, Banquo) and other evidence of the supernatural influence on human life; magic;

4. offstage action narrated by messengers;

5. choral commentary (usually a chorus of one), but chorus not integrated into the action;

6. highly passionate dialogue and soliloquies (Roman **rhetoric**);

7. often several onstage deaths; fights;

8. a five act structure;

9. the **confidante;**

10. **soliloquies & asides.**

SENEX

(Latin: "old man") A central character type in Roman comedy, the senile old man, often a miser and/or a lecher, who represents the old society which blocks the desires of the younger generation (i.e., the hero and heroine).

SENTIMENTAL COMEDY

Late 17th century English comedy of manners which developed in response to Puritan objections to the "immorality and profaneness" of comedies of the Restoration.[79] In sentimental comedy, the amoral activities of Restoration characters are replaced by the "sentiments" or values of the middle class. As the propaganda of a new ideology, sentimental comedy shifted the focus away from the "decadent" aristocracy and onto the trials of true virtue, thus evoking a "joy too exquisite for laughter" in the audience.[80]

Sentimentalism, in contrast to the (Catholic) doctrine of original sin, postulated an innate goodness in humankind. Evil behaviour was seen as a result of bad examples (an early version of the influence of environment on behaviour--see **naturalism**). Consequently, all a person needed to follow the path of righteousness was moral instruction through examples of good behaviour. This was the **social function** of all drama and theatre. The rewards of good behaviour were measured in terms of material success: in spite of all the sentiments which might be expressed, the hero and heroine were invariably rewarded with money, titles, social status and property. These characteristics, therefore, make sentimental comedy the generic ancestor of **melodrama**. (See **poetic justice**; George Lillo's *The London Merchant*, 1731; see also Colley Cibber's *Love's Last Shift*, 1696; Sir Richard Steele's *The Conscious Lovers*, 1722; Richard B. Sheridan's *The School for Scandal*, 1777--in which final act moral conversions of the hero are typical.)

(See Joseph Wood Krutch, *Comedy and Conscience after the Restoration*, 1924; Robert D. Hume, *The Development of English Drama in the Late 17th Century*, 1976; Helene Koon, *Colley Cibber, a Biography*, 1986.)

SERVUS

---

[79]Jeremy Collier, "A Short View of the Immorality and Profaneness of the English Stage," in Dukore, *Dramatic Theory and Criticism*, pp. 351-358.

[80]Sir Richard Steele, Prologue to "The Conscious Lovers" in *Plays of the Restoration and Eighteenth Century*, (London: Oxford Univ. Press, 1954), p. 549.

(Latin: "slave") The archetypal "tricky" servant from Roman comedy (see **trickster**). For such a character to become a *type*, a society with a strong class structure and an entrenched custom of using captured slaves as servants must exist. Thus, in later comedy, the wily servant may no longer have been a slave, but the role remained unchanged.

The tricky servant can be seen from two perspectives: from the master's point of view, the servant is potentially a thief and parasite and less than human; from the servant's point of view, however, being tricky is a survival strategy in a life of bondage.

SETTING

Regardless of the basic style of the production (i.e., whether **representational** or **presentational**), the setting is the location of the play's **action**. In the former case, the setting will be an illusion of another space/time actuality; in the latter case, the setting will purport to be in the "here and now" of the audience. In either case, however, the setting is a designed **code system**: even a "bare" stage requires design decisions and contributes contextual meaning.

SHAMANISM

A form of religious practice and belief dating from pre-historic times and found (in variations) among the indigenous nomadic peoples of most land masses. Shamanism is "holistic" in that the human, animal, plant and spirit worlds are believed to be interdependent, and that as a consequence, physical health is tied to spiritual health. Individual shamans thus practice both "religion" and "medicine."

The shaman practices his art and craft within a community of belief through techniques of ecstacy. In trance states the shaman travels among spirit worlds in the sky or underworld in order to communicate with the forces which influence human life. The efficacy of the shaman's healing depends on his individual powers and the belief of the community.

Since all cultures developed within either shamanistic or sedentary religious traditions (or both), scholars have recently speculated that some forms of theatre and even drama began within both traditions. While the formal religious doctrines of sedentary societies are based on coherent mythologies and communal ritual practices, shamans conduct their esoteric rituals alone (or with one or two assistants), while the community merely observes and awaits the outcome. These ritual **performances** are known to be highly theatrical, making use of costumes, masks, drums, dances and "magical" effects. While the shaman is the community healer, and while his performance is intended to heal the spirit and body of the sick, he is also the "hero" of an epic journey into the spirit world. It is therefore quite easy to appreciate the possible similarities between an audience at a play, a community observing a shaman and Aristotle's notion of **catharsis**.

(See Theodore Gaster, *Thespis: Ritual, Myth and Drama in the Ancient Near East*, 1950; Mircea Eliade, *Shamanism: Archaic Techniques of Ecstasy*, 1951; Claude Levi-Strauss, *The Savage Mind*, 1966 and *Structural Anthropology*, 1963; David Cole, *The Theatrical Event*, 1975; E.T. Kirby, *The Ur Drama: the Origins of Theatre*, 1975.)

SIDEKICK

Literally, a person standing by your side who can be kicked; an American popular term for a figure in cross-cultural legend, fiction and drama; a friend, or an assistant of inferior race and/or social class.

The sidekick is the archetypal companion of the hero, who often has powers or knowledge or abilities (thanks to his exotic background or class) which can be of use to the hero in his struggles against society or other dangers. The first sidekick in written literature was Enkidu, the companion of Gilgamesh in the Sumerian Epic (ca. 2700 BCE).[81] Enkidu was a "wild or natural man," possibly based on and representing the last of Palaeolithic culture, while Gilgamesh was a King in a

---

[81]*The Epic of Gilgamesh*, an English version by N.K. Sandars (Harmondsworth, Middlesex: Penguin, 1960).

Neolithic society. More important than either, however, was the *relationship* between them: when Enkidu died, Gilgamesh became suicidal, suggesting that he had lost half of himself:

> O Enkidu, my brother,
> You were the axe at my side,
> My hand's strength, the sword in my belt,
> The shield before me,
> A glorious robe, my fairest ornament.[82]

Sidekicks throughout the history of legend, fiction and drama were mainly important in their function as companions, and it is from this function that many gained interest as individuals. Think of Alexander and Callimachus, Arthur and Merlin, Hamlet and Horatio, Huck Finn and Jim, the Lone Ranger and Tonto. Think also, of the sidekick who is a woman disguised as a man and the sexual symbolism of the relationship becomes clear (e.g., Viola in *Twelfth Night*.).

In drama, the sidekick, as friend or servant of the hero, has appeared in both comedy and tragedy and most genres in between (e.g., Valentine and Proteus in *Two Gentlemen of Verona,* Romeo and Mercutio in *Romeo and Juliet,* Lear, the Fool and Kent in *King Lear,* Prince Hal and Falstaff in *Henry IV,* 1--in Shakespeare alone).

SIGN

A sign is a relationship between a *signifier* and a *signified*. For example, the letters **C, A, T,** are signifiers; in this configuration they signify the domestic feline, which is the signified. **Icon, index** and **symbol** are sub categories of signs. (See also: **semiotics, semantics, syntactics, pragmatics, code systems**.)

SINGSPIEL

(German: "singing play") Similar to the English **ballad opera** and the French *opera comique,* the *singspiel* is a form of music drama which flourished in Germany

---

[82]*Gilgamesh*, p. 94, 5-9.

in the early 19th century. Songs in the play were frequently mere additions marking scene breaks.

SITUATION

A term which encompasses specific circumstances, an **issue** and the characters involved. A situation is not limited to any specific dramaturgical length, such as a **french scene**, but continues until the issue is resolved or is replaced by another and the circumstances have changed..

SKENE

(Greek: "hut or tent," hence "scene building") A very controversial feature of the Greek theatre. Possibly it was originally no more than a changing room for actors and later became part of the "scene" as a palace or house. The parts of the Greek theatre (of any theatre) are of dramaturgical significance. Unfortunately, the only parts of the *fifth century* Greek theatre which have general agreement among scholars are the seating area (*theatron*), the "dancing place" (*orchestra*) and the altar (*themele*). By the *fourth century* there is more agreement on the existence and physical appearance of the *skene* and the raised platform or stage (*logeion*).

(See Peter Arnott, *Greek Scenic Conventions in the Fifth Century*, 1962.)

SLAPSTICK

Literally, a **property** constructed of two flat boards hinged near the handle so that one will slap against the other when an object (such as a character's behind) is struck, making a loud noise. By extension, then, "slapstick comedy" is usually farcical and filled with physical activity and visual/kinetic humour such as pratfalls, pies in the face etc.

SLICE OF LIFE

The full quotation is, "a play is a slice of life *artfully staged*," by Jean Jullien, one of Andre Antoine's playwrights at the Theatre Libre.[83] As a prescription for current practices, Jullien meant to describe a **naturalistic** action presented in a **realistic** style, but modified by the artistic creativity of all involved--not the artificial **well-made plays** of the commercial theatre. The phrase reminds us that such a play is not life, but life interpreted as art.

SOCIAL FUNCTION

Social function is a critical methodology which focuses primary attention on what a work of art actually *does* in and for society. Social function sees the aesthetics of a work and its reflection of its society as aspects of its *function* as an instrument which supports the ideology of its patrons. Historically, a painting, a building, musical composition or a play may have been a thing of beauty and fine craftsmanship, and it may have been an expression of the artist's sensibility, but it was also a vehicle of "conviction and persuasion."[84] Establishment arts have always been ideological statements; how convincing they have been was a function of their beauty and their appropriateness for their times.

Who commissioned Michelangelo and Raphael to paint their huge fresco programmes in the Vatican? Who dictated their subjects and general composition and for what *purpose*? Once we cut through the "great artist" theory of art, we learn that in fact these paintings were commissioned by Pope Julius II, that the programme was the work of the Pope's theological advisor, Marco Vigerio. The purpose (social function) of the work was threefold: first, to reinforce belief; second, to counter reformist heresies; and third, to serve as visual metaphors of the Pope's claim to absolute authority (the Pope's features are quite recognisable in the portraits of Old

---

[83] Jean Jullien, *The Living Theatre* (Paris: 1892), in Marvin Carlson, *Theories of the Theatre* (Ithaca: Cornell Univ. Press, 1984), p. 279.

[84] Alan Gowans, *Learning to See*, chapter V.

Testament prophets in the Sistine Ceiling).[85] (See Arnold Hauser, *The Social History of Art*, 1968 (1951).

Since the majority of dramatic works *which have survived* were products of political and/or ecclesiastical patronage, it should not be surprising that their social function supported the ideological programmes of those patrons. This applies equally to the tragedies of Sophocles under the rule of Pericles, to the **mysteries** of the Wakefield cycle under the supervision of the English church, and to the histories, tragedies and comedies of Shakespeare and his contemporaries under the patronage of the Tudors and Stuarts.

But what of the arts since **romanticism**? The romantic artist often refused patronage because he would not allow his "vision" to be compromised. With the romantics, art had become *primarily* a matter of personal expression. If we apply social function to modern works of personal expression preserved in galleries, libraries and universities, however, we can see that they tend to be **avant garde**, supported and enjoyed by a tiny fraction of the population. The popular and commercially viable arts of the same period, from theatrical entertainment to advertising, from serial novels and best sellers to cartoons and from motion pictures to TV sitcoms, however, continue to serve traditional social functions.[86]

The theory of social function requires that this perspective be foremost in our critical methodologies when we examine either historical arts or the popular commercial arts of our own times. This does not preclude formal analysis or even critical judgement, but it does condition these responses. (See also **deconstruction.**)

SOCIALIST REALISM

An attempt, on the part of the Soviet Ministry of Culture in the 1930's to

---

[85]Ibid., pp. 74; 270 f. See also, Frederick Hartt, "The Stanza d'Eliodoro and the Sistine Ceiling," *Art Bulletin*, XXXII, 1950, p. 214.

[86]Alan Gowans, *Learning to See*, chapter V.

identify and then impose a socialist vocabulary (a **style**) on the form and content of all Soviet art. Non-realist styles (e.g., **expressionism, symbolism**) were seen as products of western "decadence," which was not so much a moral as a cultural criticism. If the theory of **social function** is rigorously applied to this situation, it is clear that such a programme does no more than make explicit the functions of all traditional arts, much in the way academies of the Renaissance and Baroque periods did with the "rules" of **neoclassicism**. Further, the critique of modern western art as "decadent" simply draws attention to the split between individualist (socially "useless") **avant garde** arts and the popular commercial arts, which may be decadent in another sense: that is, materialist and hedonistic.

(See Georg Lukacs, *Studies in European Realism*, 1964; Terry Eagleton, *Marxism and Literary Criticism*, 1976 and *Walter Benjamin, or Toward a Revolutionary Criticism*, 1981.)

SOLILOQUY

A solo speech, that is, the performer is alone on stage, as opposed to a **monologue**, where others may be present. Dramaturgically, the soliloquy functioned as a **convention** in which the playwright could expose a character's thoughts and feelings. (See also **aria**.) In **presentational theatre**, the soliloquy facilitates performer/ character/audience intimacy.

SOUND EFFECT

An aural **code** which may occur on stage as a direct part of the action, or off stage as a manifestation of **offstage life**. Sound effects are practically infinite in their potential variety, as they include every type of sound heard by the audience except speech, song and music. In general usage, however, the term applies to offstage sounds made to imitate certain effects, such as thunder and rain, gun shots, doors closing, footsteps, crowd noises and so on.

SPEECH

The primary aural **code** of **drama**; one of the actor's fundamental means of communication. Speech is so fundamental a characteristic of the human condition as a function of social relationships, that its absence on stage (e.g., **mime**) can be shockingly effective.

Dramaturgically, as an imitation of human discourse, dramatic speech can appear in a number of styles, from highly structured and elevated poetry to fragments of semi-coherence, from a measure of a specific social class and/or character to a generalized style (which includes accents). Playwrights must therefore make a number of fundamental choices in speech style which will affect the dramaturgy of character relationships:

1. Will some or all characters speak in verse or prose?

2. Will some or all characters speak in syntactically correct sentences or in semi-coherent fragments?

3. Will the characters all speak in the same style/dialect or will the speech of each character reflect his/her class, education, gender and/or profession?

4. Will the speech be colloquial and contemporaneous with the audience or from another time and place?

Such choices will determine the degree of communication possible between characters. If they all speak the same "language," communication will not be an **issue** of either the dramaturgy or the **action**. This is one reason why plays from the 16th through the 19th centuries often had persons of lower class in the cast of characters--their speech style provided a sharp contrast (and thus vindication) to the elite norm. On the other hand, communication may be the key issue if some of the characters cannot relate in terms of speech style and/or vocabulary. For example, teenagers and parents, workers and employers, academics and students, business people and artists--all failing to communicate on a meaningful level can become a major issue in a play.

STAGE DIRECTIONS

Stage directions should be distinguished from **scene directions**. The former refer to the following; the latter to directions for blocking etc. written into the script by the playwright or text editors. Stage directions map the geography of the playing surface of the stage for the convenience of actors, directors and designers. Such directions are always referred to from the **pov** of the actor facing the audience.

STAGE DIRECTIONS

UP RIGHT UR	UP CENTRE UC	UP LEFT UL
RIGHT CENTRE RC	CENTRE C	LEFT CENTRE LC
DOWN RIGHT DR	DOWN CENTRE DC	DOWN LEFT DL

STAGE MACINERY

Since the ancient Greeks (at least), the technical means of production, including not only the seating area and the stage itself, but special "machines" or mechanical means of changing scenery, bringing actors and objects on and off stage and so on have been major considerations of **production dramaturgy**. Such machines range from the *deus ex machina* to the *ekkyklema*, from the wing and drop system to the revolve and hydraulic traps. All affect the manner in which the producers create the special illusion of the performance and in turn the way the audience receives the performance.

STASIMON

(Greek: "stance") In Greek tragedy, the ode sung (and danced) by the **chorus** between **episodes**. Each *stasimon* is usually divided into two parts (*"strophe"* or movement and *"anti-strophe,"* or counter movement), one for each half of the chorus. Such a division is actually an embedded **code** indicating at least one aspect of the visual/kinetic performance. The two parts of the *stasimon* are also marked by differences in tone, argument and choral style, and this too may have influenced the style of speech and movement. *Stasima* are concluded with a (motionless) *epode*.

STICHOMYTHIA

(Greek: "telling a story, line by line") A formal dialogue style, appearing first in Greek tragedy, but adopted by Seneca and later the Elizabethans. In a duet, the characters alternate with short lines and this results in a section of fast, sharp dialogue.

STORY THEATRE

Almost a contradiction in terms, story theatre attempts to combine **performance** with **narrative**; in turn, parts of the narrative may be dramatized with character dialogue (i.e., in the present). One of the results of this technique is that it allows the playwright to set the performance in the present, but the action in the past and to switch back and forth between the two dimensions.

Story Theatre is also the name of a style of improvisational theatre developed by the American director Paul Sills (son of Viola Spolin: *Improvisation for the Theatre*, 1963) in the 1960's. In this style, actors assume various characters and drop them as the needs of the "story" requires.

STRATEGY

A term which describes both a character's **objective** and the means employed to reach it. A strategy is comprised of **tactics**, which can be seen as "mini strategies." Robert Cohen uses the analogy of the slalom skier to describe the relationship between the two: the skier has an overall plan to reach the finish line as fast as possible, but each gate along the way has its specific problems which require individual tactical responses. In such situations, the gates become the skier's **obstacles**, which must be overcome if the objective is to be achieved. It should be noted that tactics, strategies, obstacles and objectives are all aids to character and script analysis before and during the rehearsal period. The actual character may not be aware of some of them most of the time. (See Robert Cohen, *Acting Power*, 1978.)

STROPHE / ANTI STROPHE

Movement and counter movement in a choral ode (see *stasimon*).

STRUCTURALISM

An analytic strategy and theory of cultural meaning, structuralism originated in linguistics and anthropology. The central notion is that meaning resides in *relationships*: in linguistics the conjunction of a signifier and a signified produces a meaningful **sign**; in anthropology the structure of a myth, in which parts relate to each other and to the whole, reveals deep social meaning with cross-cultural implications.

Structural analysis has particular relevance to both **drama** and **theatre**. The importance of a scene lies in the relationships within it (characters and **issues**) and its relationships with the scenes before and after and with the **action** as a whole. The importance of a character lies in his/her relationships with other characters; the importance of a **property** lies in its relationship to character/scene/situation and so on. In short, insofar as a work of art is a coherent whole, the relations of its parts to each other and to the whole produce meaning.

(See Claude Levi-Strauss, *Structural Anthropology*, 1963; R. Macksey, ed. *The Structuralist Controversy*, 1972; Jonathan Culler, *Structuralist Poetics*, 1975; John Sturrock, ed., *Structuralism and After: From Levi-Strauss to Derrida*, 1979.)

STURM UND DRANG

(German: "storm and stress) A pre-romantic movement in German theatre and literature which set itself against the rules of **neoclassicism**. The movement had an undertone of early German nationalism, for neoclassicism was perceived as a foreign (French) imposition. Theoretically, the movement was opposed by Goethe and Schiller (see **Weimar classicism**), but the major works of these great playwrights can hardly be classed as neoclassic. Goethe's *Faust (1808)* and Schiller's *Mary Stuart (1800)*, for example, are milestones of **romanticism**.

STYLE

The word is overused and therefore misused. In the theatre style refers to characteristic behaviour in an individual ("personal style"), an overall uniformity of behaviour in a play (Cohen's "collective characterization"[87]), or a set of related **conventions** in playwriting or performance (e.g., those which may result in a **representational** or a **presentational** "style"). Finally, acting "style" refers to the characteristic relationships between the actor, the text, the role and the audience (or camera). One need only compare Lawrence Olivier's *Hamlet* with Mel Gibson's to appreciate the wide range of acting style possible even in motion pictures of the same play.

In painting and scene design, style might include a specific technique which affects both the form and content of the work: the impasto style, for example, with a highly textured surface and visible brush or knife strokes. In music, characteristic structures such as the sonata form, orchestrations or key change techniques result in styles.

(See also Michel St. Denis, *Theatre: a Rediscovery of Style*, 1960.)

---

[87]Robert Cohen, *Acting Power* (Irvine: Mayfield, 1979), chapter four.

SUB PLOT

A subordinate plot line which usually serves to foreground the main plot by contrast, analogy or change of perspective as does the "Gloucester plot" in Shakespeare's *King Lear*. (See also **double plot**.)

SUBTEXT

The underlying meaning or intention of a line of dialogue; the inner life of a character, which can only be inferred through observing behaviour in a variety of relationships. Subtext is communicated through body language, gesture and vocal inflection or emphasis. *Any reading of a line* therefore infers a subtext, but it is the business of the actor to make this subtext coherent and unified. Subtext is an aspect of **performance dramaturgy**: as Stanislavsky is purported to have said, "I can read the text at home; I go to the theatre for the subtext." (See also **relacom**.)

One of the major developments in playwrighting since the ancient Greeks has been in the area of subtext. Before the 19th century, characters usually said more or less what they meant. If they wanted to express feelings and ideas, but outside of their normal relationships, they told confidantes or sidekicks, or they spoke to the audience (**asides**), or they simply expressed their feelings aloud when alone on stage (**solioquy, aria**). With the modern turn toward **realism**, however, most of theses **conventions** were no longer acceptable and they were **displaced** into the dialogue as subtext.

SURREALISM

"Beyond realism;" a movement in painting. literature and the theatre which attempted to break through the empirical fixation of **realism** and the determinism of **naturalism** by suggesting the importance of unconscious drives, the inspiration of dreams, the creative potential of chance in life and art. The term was first used by Guillaume Apollinaire in connection with the production of Jean Cocteau's *Parade* in 1917 in which apparently random juxtapositions of objects and images were highly suggestive. Later Apollinaire applied the term to describe the aesthetic **conventions** of his *The Breasts of Tiresias*, 1918.

The first surrealist "manifesto," written by Andre Breton (the self-proclaimed leader of the movement) in 1924, applied the theories of Freud to the creative act, arguing that such acts are spontaneous and that they precede cognition. This led to experiments in "automatic writing" and writing under hypnosis--attempts to bypass the logical structures of the conscious mind.

The impact of surrealism is only now being felt in the theatre through the influence of the works of Antonin Artaud *(The Theatre and its Double*, 1938) and **absurdism** or recent **post modern** experiments with disconnected stage images (see **performance art**). Umberto Eco has coined the term "hyperrealism" to denote works of art, such as the works of the "photorealists" which have a "reality so real that (they) proclaim (their) artificiality from the rooftops."[88] Artifacts of modern popular culture such as the properties and buildings in Disneyworld or replicas of the President's oval office duplicate an original exactly, but are placed in contexts where their falseness is evident. This is a modern extension of **realism** which throws the whole notion of "reality" (of such concern of philosophers since Plato and Aristotle) into serious question once again. It is at this point that art becomes "meta-art" and surreal.

(See Andre Breton, *What is Surrealism?* 1936; C. Schumacher, *Alfred Jarry and Guillaume Apollinaire,* 1985.)

SYMBOL

A symbol is a conventional **sign**: for example, by **convention** the cross symbolizes the crucifixion, although there is no necessary connection between them. The letters of the alphabet are conventional symbols. (See **semiotics**.)

---

[88]Umberto Eco, *Travels in Hyperreality: Essays*, trans. by William Weaver (London: Harcourt Brace Jovanovitch, 1986, 1976), p. 7.

SYMBOLISM

A specific movement in literature and the theatre which attempted to use the **conventions** of words and images to suggest meaning beyond appearance. To the symbolists of late 19th century France, the Truth of anything could only be suggested: once "named" or made concrete, it became limited to the real-- contaminated by its finite existence. Words on the page and words and images on the stage were used to signify images-behind-images (second degree signifieds) through implication, ambiguity and the atmosphere of context. These were attempts to express the mysterious forces of life beyond mere signification. One conclusion from these experiments was that music was the perfect bridge between this mystery and life because music totally bypasses rational thought: "all art aspires toward the condition of music."[89]

Beginning with *Brand,* and *Peer Gynt* and on a more sophisticated level with *The Wild Duck* and *Rosmersholm,* Ibsen's language suggests meaning on increasingly complex planes of existence. The wild duck itself, for example, has a material existence and a detailed history, but by implication in a variety of contexts, the duck and its "history" begin to symbolize characters and their relationships to each other. Similarly, literal blindness in one character applies figuratively to others; photography, which provides the family with a meagre livelihood, begins to symbolize the relation between the ideal (artificial) and the real; frequent lighting **codes** begin to imply sight and blindness and so on through an intricate web of second and third degree signification.

Since a symbol is a **conventional sign**, however, there can be a twofold problem with symbolist works: either the convention is made too obvious, or it is not made at all and the work loses symbolic coherence. The "dream plays" of August Strindberg, for example, are filled with symbolism of a very personal and/or esoteric

---

[89]Walter Pater, *The Renaissance: Studies in Art and Poetry* (London: Oxford Univ. Press, 1910), p. 136.

nature to which most audiences have no access.

The leading symbolist in the theatre was Maurice Maeterlink (1862-1949: see *The Intruder*, 1890, *The Blind*, 1890, *Pelleas and Melisande*, 1892). (See also, Frantisek Deak, *Symbolist Theatre: the Formation of the Avant Garde*, 1993.)

SYNAESTHESIA

(Greek: "to perceive simultaneously") The idea that certain sense impressions can trigger impressions in other senses: for example, a sound can trigger a colour response; colours can evoke sensations of heat or cold. At various times in the history of the arts similar ideas supported efforts to relate one medium with others. Composers wrote "tone poems" and painters saw their works as "frozen music." In literature synaesthesia is often used metaphorically in attempts to evoke similar responses in the reader.

SYNCHRONIC

(Greek: "at the same time") Events happening at the same time; an event in its present context. For example, a theatrical production of *Hamlet* in the context of the prevailing ideology and concurrent events. A production of *Hamlet* in 1994 is quite different from a productions of *Hamlet* in 1954 or 1854 merely because of their synchronic contexts. Theatrical events do not occur in cultural vacuums: the analysis of a production must take its ideological context into account. (See **diachronic**.)

SYNERGY

(Greek: "working together") "The effect of a whole system will be greater than the sum of its parts or any sub-assembly of parts."[90] When structures which normally have little to do with each other are combined to form an integral whole, a synthesis occurs which creates a new form at a higher level of complexity. In

---

[90] R. Buckminster Fuller, *Synergetics* (London: MacMillan, 1975), p. 68.

physics, for example, the alloy created by the combination of chrome, nickel and steel is far stronger than any one of them or the three together.

Synergy in this sense is the major principle behind theatre as a **multi-modal communication system**. Modes of communication (such as speech and painting) which normally function separately are combined as a more powerful single art. In other words, by combining information on three channels simultaneously (aural, visual and kinetic), a higher, more complex level of communication can occur than through one channel at a time. This implies that simultaneity is more than merely additive ("sum of the parts"). Part of the effect is a result of the workings of human perception, emotion, creativity and cognition between all involved, from playwright to audience; another part is created by the effect of **redundancy** and a constantly shifting hierarchy of channels (the theatrical synergy is *dynamic*); a final part results from the combination of time arts (speech, music and movement) and space arts (settings, costumes, properties).

SYNTACTICS

(Greek: "arranging together") The functional relationships between signs and by extension between the parts of any system. In the following simple sentence, for example:

THE BOY HIT THE BALL

the individual words ("boy," "hit" and "ball") are **signs** (the relationships between the signifiers and signifieds); the relationships between these words in this order are grammatical, that is, syntactical: "boy" is a noun, "hit" is the verb and "ball" is the object.

In the theatrical event, the syntactical relations between the modes or channels of communication (aural, visual and kinetic) are dramaturgical. In other words, the focus of analysis is on the relationships between, for example, speech and movement, or between the setting and moving actors and background music, and so on.

SYSTEMIC CHANGE

Any readily perceptible change in the quantity and/or quality of aural, visual and/or kinetic communication systems on the stage. Within a **french scene**, for example, a shift from speech to song, the occurrence of sound effects or offstage dialogue, a sudden change in lighting or scenery, the sudden intrusion of an object (such as a rock through a window), and above all, the entrance or exit of a character *are all systemic changes.*

Systemic changes must of course be noted in script analysis and in the **performance text**. If a french scene contains a systemic change, it is no longer a "stable" unit for analysis, but in theory should be subdivided into periods of time on stage *in which there are no systemic changes.*

This is a rule, however, which can be taken to impractical extremes: technically, a spoken line is a change from the momentary silence preceding it, a small gesture is a change from the stillness preceding it and so on. Semiotic analyses of texts and performances can be overwhelmed by such considerations (see Kier Elam, *The Semiotics of Theatre and Drama*, 1980). Consequently, semioticians and dramaturges tend to focus on the french scene and its divisions into **beats** (that is, a focus on **character**) and simply note major systemic changes and their effects on subsequent action.

T

TABLEAU VIVANT

(French: "living picture") A stage picture with stationary actors which illustrates a dramatic moment, a moral, or an historical event; figures on a parade float; a dramatic "snap shot." Tableaus were popular in **pageants** during the Corpus Christi Festival and from the late 18th and most of the 19th centuries as dramatic Act-ending stage pictures. In the latter case, the tableau was often revealed *after* the Act curtain had fallen as an "Act call"--in other words, the tableau was an added feature, not simply a frozen moment already seen in action. (See Tom Robertson's *Caste*, for example.)

TACTICS

Robert Cohen's term for the moment to moment choices an actor/character makes in pursuing an **objective**.[91] If an objective is a character's goal, and a **strategy** his or her overall plan to achieve that goal, a tactic defines a **beat** of the strategy: when the character decides to try a different tactic (or does so unconsciously), the beat changes. If **character** is defined by what a person actually does, tactics define character.

According to Cohen, there are just two general types of tactics, "threat" and "induction." The former includes all those actions designed to place the Other (character) in a defensive position and correspondingly to maximize one's authority.

---

[91] Robert Cohen. *Acting Power* (Irvine: Mayfield, 1979), chapter two.

The actor/character does this in a wide variety of ways, from raising the voice and/or fist to using sarcasm, from relative body position to characterizing the Other as inferior. The latter type, in contrast, attempts to provide the Other with an "inducement" to cooperate, that is, a "win-win" option. A simple smile is such an inducement; using reason, flattery, bribery and countless similar tactics help one create a positive relationship with the Other. Some tactics are deliberate parts of a conscious strategy; often they are simply unconscious responses (of the character) to the tactics of the Other.

TEXTUAL DRAMATURGY

Textual dramaturgy is concerned with the embedded **code systems** of a play script, all of which will affect performance directly or indirectly. Textual dramaturgy is thus a matter of playwright choices, the means used to influence the eventual production: everything from the size and composition of the cast to the size, composition and duration of **french scenes**; from embedded **business** and **properties** to the evocation of **offstage life**; from the structural use of exposition to the relation of **plot** (form) to **action** (content).

The dramaturgical analysis of a text is intended to expose and explain the embedded codes as part of the creation of a **performance text**. Some means of tabulating, correlating and comparing dramaturgical data is a necessary first step (see **figures 6-8**).

(See Manfred Pfister, *The Theory and Analysis of Drama*, 1988.)

THEATRE

A multi purpose term (a building, an institution, a tradition, an event) which must be distinguished from **drama** (a text). The theatre *event* implies **performance** and **presence**, involving a physical configuration between performer(s) and audience. It is an event, moreover, which may or may not include drama, but does include musical and dance performances, lectures and sports (for example). The theatrical event brings performer(s) and audience together *by mutual consent*, thus creating a "community" through a shared experience. Bruce A. McConachie goes further by defining theatre "as a type of ritual which functions to legitimate an image of historical social order . . . ."[92] By adding this dimension to the definition, McConachie includes a necessary consideration of theatre's **social function**.

Theatre architecture, the central focus of **production dramaturgy**, influences the dramaturgy of the events it shelters through size, seating arrangements, audience/performer configurations, stage equipment, **lobby** space and facilities and so on. The history of the theatre is thus partly the history of the evolution of theatre spaces, from the huge Greek open aired **theatron** to the intimate **cabaret** of pre war Berlin, from opulent baroque opera houses to converted **fringe** theatres.

THEATRE GAMES

Games played using the dramaturgy of performance usually as training aids and/or improvisational techniques. The purpose is to prepare actors for spontaneous interaction in performance. In the past 25 years theatre games of various kinds have been elevated to actual performance (see **theatre sports**).

(See Viola Spolin, *Improvisation for the Theatre*, 1963; *Theatre Games for Rehearsal*, 1985.)

THEATRE HISTORY

Theatre History as a formal academic discipline is relatively new. Most theatre history was studied and researched under different auspices, such as departments of Literature. Oscar Brockett's *History of the Theatre*, now in its sixth edition, was first published in 1968. It was preceded (as a college text in North America) by John Gassner's *Masters of the Drama* (first published in 1940), which, as the title implies, focused on people--mainly playwrights. Before that Allardyce Nicoll's *The Development of the Theatre* (1927) and Sheldon Cheney's *The Theatre:*

---

[92]"Towards a Postpositivist Theatre History," in *Theatre Journal*, December, 1985, p. 466.

Three Thousand Years of Acting, Drama and Stagecraft (1929) were the only serious histories of the subject.

In the post war era the study of Theatre History as a discipline distinct from **drama** has become widespread. Theatre history is now seen as the history of the interrelationships of the branches of **dramaturgy** (text, performance, production and reception) and **social function**. No longer the study of "masterpieces" and "genius," or of an "evolution" of forms and techniques from the primitive to the sophisticated, theatre history is essentially interested in all of the artistic and social circumstances surrounding the productions of specific plays and other theatrical events.

How such data is gathered and interpreted have become matters of some debate. Because the theatrical event is a crucible of culture, encompassing every aspect of a society's values, traditions, knowledge and skills, the relationships among its parts has become crucial. One way to visualize the problem is to see the theatrical event as a series of concentric circles, with the idea/text relationship at the centre, the performance/society relationship at the outer edge, and all other relationships arranged in between. Some would argue, however, that the actor/audience relationship should be central, with the text at the outer edge as mere documentation. Others would say that the general relationship between theatre and society is central, with specific events and issues being merely peripheral.

(See Oscar Brockett, *History of the Theatre,* sixth edition, 1992; Bruce A. McConachie, "Towards a Postpositivist Theatre History," in *Theatre Journal,* December, 1985, pp. 465-487.)

THEATRE OF THE ABSURD

(See **absurdism**)

THEATRE OF CRUELTY

A phrase first coined by Antoinin Artaud (1896-1948) to describe a theatre which would confront its audience with itself and thus purge its repressions and violence: "the theatre has been created to drain abscesses collectively."[93] Stripped of the literary and philosophical trappings of western theatre, the theatre of cruelty was to mount a direct assault on the psyche through ritual, sound, dance and mime. It is a manifesto calling for an end of the "polite theatre" of language and a return to the primitive theatre of gesture and scream. This is what was meant by the theatre and its "double."

Artaud, originally an actor and surrealist painter/director, belongs to the extreme **avant garde** of early 20th century theatre, but his influence on various directors, writers and alternative styles has been enormous. The most famous interpretation of Artaud's vision was Peter Brook's production of Peter Weiss's *Marat/Sade* in 1964.

(See Peter Brook, *The Empty Space*, 1968; Jerzy Grotowski, *Towards a Poor Theatre*, 1968; Albert Bermel, *Artaud's Theatre of Cruelty*, 1978; Timothy J. Wiles, *The Theatrical Event: Modern Theories of Performance*, 1980.)

THEATRE OF IMAGES

A phrase coined by Bonnie Marranca in the title of her book on the works of modern American **alternative theatre** artists such as Robert Wilson, Lee Breuer and Richard Foreman.[94] Theatre of images describes an anti-literary tendency in alternative theatre since **Dada** and **Happenings** in which the spoken word (let alone the written word) is fragmented and cut off from its syntactic contexts. More importantly, spoken discourse becomes incidental to stage pictures created by the human body, by properties and scenery and by projections. The aural channel in theatre of images remains important, but it is often recorded in the form of background music, sound effects and fragmentary voice-overs. The theatre of images is the performance equivalent of the *collage*. (See **performance art**.)

---

[93]Antoinin Artaud, *The Theatre and its Double*, trans. by Mary C. Richards (New York: Grove Press, 1958).

[94]Bonnie Marranca, *Theatre of Images* (New York: Performing Arts Books, 1977).

THEATRE OF THE OPPRESSED

The title of a book (and a movement) by Brazilian director, Augusto Boal.[95] The book combines an ideological critique of "establishment" theatre and its place in the western tradition as a tool of cultural hegemony and provides an introduction to his experimental work in **Popular Theatre**. The fundamental **social function** of the theatre of the oppressed is *empowerment* through education: empowerment of the participants and of the audience. Boal's theatre therefore mobilizes groups within specific communities of oppressed people to express themselves and their social problems theatrically.

THEATRESPORTS

The name given to a specific form of improvisational theatre (to distinguish it from the **theatre games** of Viola Spolin) by Sheila Shanahan and Wayne Poncia (*Teaching Theatresports; The Theatresports Actors' Manual*--currently out of print). Using teams of performer/contestants, a simple set of rules (borrowed from sports and games) and referees, the basic idea is to compete for points by improvising on themes, ideas, words, situations etc. suggested by the audience. Points are often awarded by the audience through applause.

THEATRICAL IRONY

(See **dramatic irony**) Theatrical irony depends on the audience's perception of the paradox in the dramaturgy of a specific performance. This is a paradox at the heart of most theatre, but one which is foregrounded in **metatheatre**: we are asked to believe in the actuality of a fictional world conducted in obviously artificial circumstances. Samuel Taylor Coleridge called this "the willing suspension of disbelief," when applied to traditional illusionistic theatre.[96] When the audience is

---

[95]Augusto Boal, *Theatre of the Oppressed* New York: Theatre Comm. Group, 1985).

[96]S. T. Coleridge, "Biographia Literaria," III, 6, in Dukore, *Theory and Criticism*, p. 584.

forcibly reminded of the paradox as part of the performance, however, an ironic perspective is gained. Most metatheatrical devices, such as the "play-within-the-play," produce theatrical irony (see especially Pirandello's *Six Characters in Search of an Author*, 1923). More recently, the dramaturgy of Brecht's **epic theatre** aims to create an ironic objectivity in the audience through *verfremdungseffekt*. Most of the plays of Tom Stoppard create theatrical irony through several self-reflective techniques (see *The Real Inspector Hound*, 1968; *Jumpers*, 1972; *Travesties*, 1974 and *The Real Thing*, 1982).

THEATRICAL METAPHOR

A metaphor which depends on **performance** rather than text alone (as does the **dramatic metaphor**) for its complete appreciation. Such a metaphor would necessarily be **metatheatrical**. The new leaves on the lone tree in the second Act of *Waiting for Godot*, for example, are used metaphorically (an "impossible" stage prop signifying the passage of time). More profoundly in the same play, however, performance itself becomes a metaphor for human action. The characters perform individually for themselves and collectively for us as a strategy to pass the time.

THEATRICAL RELATIONSHIPS

(See **figures 2 and 3**) Beginning with the relationship between a central idea and the dramatic text which grows from it, the complex, multi-layered "meaning" of the theatrical event is the product of many interdependent relationships. Such relationships as that between an actor and his role or between a character and his behaviour; between one actor and another or between one character and another are all significant because they produce meaning. For example, it makes a difference whether an actor approaches his role technically and objectively or emotionally and subjectively; similarly, it makes a difference if a character's behaviour is written according to type or according to the principles of **naturalism**. In a theatre company it makes a difference if the actors consider each other as equals or if the stars treat each other with jealousy and the supporting cast as servants. Analogous behaviour can be observed in the characters of different plays: in one, all may be from the same social class; in another, there may be a strong contrast between masters and servants.

As can be seen from the list and the diagram, such relationships ultimately extend to much wider levels of social and artistic interaction to the point where they *define culture*. This is the case, for example, in the relationship between a specific performance, say, of *Hamlet* in London in 1994 and a history of productions of *Hamlet* in London, back to the original at the Globe Theatre in 1601. (This is a comparison of the **synchronic** and **diachronic** dimensions of a work.) Many in the current audience will recall other London productions of this play; some critics and scholars in attendance may at least have heard of several others. In either case, appreciation of this *Hamlet* will be conditioned by awareness of previous performances. All of these London productions, however, will be culturally different from a history of French productions of *Phedre* in Paris.

THEATRON

(Greek: "seeing place") The seating area of the Greek theatre (see the Roman **auditorium,** "hearing place"). The etymology suggests that the primary channel or mode of communication was visual: a place where the chorus danced and the characters were seen first and heard second.

THESIS PLAY

Attempts in the mid 19th century to write plays about the social problems of the class structured state. These plays were intended to argue a "thesis," that is, the playwright's point of view was clearly articulated by his *raisonneur*. (See Alexandre Dumas fils' *Le Demi Monde*, 1855; Emile Augier, *Olympe's Marriage*, 1855.)

Generally considered to be historical antecedents of the **naturalistic** plays of the next generation, thesis plays merely raised the subject of class only to reaffirm middle-class values at the end. (See also Tom Robertson's *Caste*, 1867, the English version of the same thesis.)

THRUST STAGE

A modern term used to differentiate between an apron stage, which merely extends the playing surface a few feet beyond the proscenium arch, and a stage which extends far enough into the auditorium to affect seating. While the term is modern, the stage type is ancient: the Greek theatre and the Elizabethan public playhouse both had audience on three sides, for example.

Dramaturgically, the thrust stage was intended to create more intimacy with the audience while retaining the possibility of a **representational style**, scenery and upstage entrances. This type of staging became popular once it was understood that the illusion created by **realism** does not depend on a retreat behind a **proscenium arch** as a picture frame, but that it can be maintained by the **conventions** of performance. On the other hand, the thrust stage also facilitated a **presentational** style when desired.

THYMELE

(Greek: "altar") Placed in the centre of the **orchestra**, probably for ceremonies and sacrifices to mark the opening of dramatic festivals, the *thymele* was either removed for performances or perhaps used in some plays as a convenient prop (see Aeschylus' *Prometheus Bound*, ca. 468 BCE).[97]

The *thymele* had equally important symbolic significance which tied the religious ritual of the festival, the theatrical performances and the Greek community together and at the same time underlines the cultural importance of **theatre** to most cultures. The *thymele* functioned symbolically as an *axis mundi,* or world axis. For the duration of the festival, the centre of the orchestra, which marked the centre of

---

[97]Peter Arnott, *Greek Scenic Conventions in the Fifth Century B.C.* (Westport, Conn.: Greenwood Press, 1962), p 44f, disagrees with the idea that the *thymele* (at least the one dedicated to Dionysus) was ever used as a prop or scenic piece, as this, he claims, would have been sacrilege.

the theatre space, was the centre of the "world" and the theatre itself consequently a sacred space. In this space, the Greek community "communed" with its culture heroes and gods *through the agency of the chorus.*

The notion of the *axis mundi* is practically universal and has appeared in many guises in different religions, from the Christian cross to the "tree of life" to the ladder at the centre of the earth. In all cases, however, it marks the place where mortals (often through intermediaries, such as shamans) can communicate with the other two planes of existence, the heavens and the underground.[98]

TIME

The theatrical event's most defining characteristics are **presence** (both performer(s) and audience are *here*) and **time** (the event passes as we observe). Combined, these two characteristics result in an *event*, that is, performers and audience are not just here, they are here now: stage time (regardless of attempts to deceive) is in fact audience time.

If the **action** of a play is confined to a very restricted period of time as urged by Aristotle and the humanists, time is not a serious factor, or at least not an active agent of the action. The thinking was that even though an illusion of another actuality has been created on the stage, the audience's sense of the passage of time would not be a problem if the action was confined to a few hours. (The flaw in this thinking becomes apparent the moment more time than actual playing time [audience time] is given to the action--12 hours is as unbelievable as 24 if the play only lasts three.)

On the other hand, if the action occurs over a relatively long period of time (months or years, for example), that time becomes a direct factor in the action: characters age, attitudes and **objectives** change, situations change and several

---

[98]Mircea Eliade, *Shamanism: Archaic Techniques of Ecstasy*, trans. by Willard R. Trask (New Jersey: Princeton Univ. Press, 1964), chapter eight. See also Joseph Campbell, *The Mythic Image* (New Jersey: Princeton Univ. Press, 1974), chapter two; S.G.F. Brandon, *Man and God in Art and Ritual: a Study of Iconography, Architecture and Ritual Action as Primary Evidence of Religious Belief and Practice* (New York: Scribner's, 1975), Part Two.

locations can be used (making space an agent of the action as well). If the characters are **naturalistically** conceived (i.e., as products of environment and heredity), they have pasts which influence the present, and each character's present is future oriented. Further, time-as-sequence is structural, whether the playwright decides to hold to a strict causality or to use "flashbacks," blank periods or simultaneous action. Sophocles' *Oedipus* does not begin **ab ovo**, but **in media res**; nevertheless, the sequence of the events of Oedipus' life, seen through sections of **exposition**, influences the structure of the action.

Finally, as noted above, time and space are *relative*: as time passes, space changes; conversely, space conditions the quality of time. As such, both time and space are agents of the action and together constitute a powerful dramaturgical mechanism. In Chekhov's *The Cherry Orchard* (1903), for example, the action begins in May and ends in October. In that time characters appear in four settings-- the first and last are the same room, but physical changes have occurred. In the beginning the cherry orchard is in bloom, at the end it is being cut down. Act two occurs out-of-doors, and this creates a very different mood and pace. The nursery room in Acts one and four is merely the momentary meeting place of many characters who pass through on their way to other spaces. In Act one several people arrive from Paris; in Act four most are departing for a number of places. Overall, time is demonstrated to have had an effect on characters, their relationships with each other and with their environment (both near and far). Each character is seen to have a past and hopes for the future, both of which influence the present. Each character has a specific relationship to the estate, and this relationship is conditioned by each character's past, present, and future.

TOURNAMENT

A militaristic sport which began as competitive jousts for the training of knights during the middle ages, but which became highly theatrical performances with music, pageantry and contestants in allegorical disguises.[99] Tournaments were usually a major feature of courtly festivals, preceded by colourful parades and followed by lavish banquets with entertainment. (As such, tournaments were antecedents of the "contest" of **festive theatre**: see **figure 12**.)

As displaced festive contests, tournaments can be seen in the evolution of Tudor **masques**: tournament pageants and scenic devices were actually wheeled indoors as part of the banquet's entertainment.[100]

(See Otto Cartellieri, *The Court of Burgundy*, 1970; Richard Vaughan, *Valois Burgundy*, 1975.)

TOTAL THEATRE

(See *gesamkunstwerk* and **figure 12**)

TRAGEDY

(See **figure 1: "The Ur Drama, Fall**) Generically, tragedy is the polar opposite of **comedy**.[101] Its basis in **ritual** and **myth** is the sacrificed god/king ("scapegoat"), whose death is seen as a communal purgation. A tragedy is about an individual whose stubborn pursuit of a personal vision (desire, ambition) sets him/herself apart from the community he/she represents. Theoretically this individual can be male or female, king or commoner; in traditional practice tragic heroes have been aristocratic and male. Taking such a position inevitably ends in death, banishment or some form of fall from a higher position. Tragedy is fundamentally serious. Nevertheless, tragedy and comedy can be seen as two views of the same human predicament: the relationship of an individual to the group.

---

[99]For a detailed description of such a tournament, see Froissart's *Chronicles* (ca. 1400), trans. by Geoffrey Brereton (Harmondsworth, Middlesex: Penguin, 1968), Book Four, "Tournament at Saint-Inglevert, (1390)" pp. 373-381. See also, Sidney Anglo, *Spectacle, Pageantry and Early Tudor Policy* (London: Thames and Hudson, 1969).

[100]Anglo, *Spectacle, Pageantry and Early Tudor Policy*, pp. 101-103.

[101]Northrop Frye, *Anatomy of Criticism*, Third Essay, "Archetypal Criticism."

Tragedies generally have been concerned with the traditions, values and problems of the elite and not, like comedy, with the foibles of the lower classes. There have been exceptions which prove the rule: Restoration comedies are mainly about the idle rich, but most have comic servants, while **domestic tragedies** are little more than middle-class cautionary tales. Tragedy is not about the lives of dynamic middle-class characters poised as individuals and as a class on the cusp of power. Rather, it is about an aristocracy which sees itself as having slipped from the glory of a golden age.

The point to bear in mind when considering the characteristics of all genres is that they represent accepted norms (or **displacements**) of specific times and places and as such are unavoidably and fundamentally ideological. Greek tragedy is about a Greek oligarchy which mourns and celebrates its heroic past; Elizabethan tragedy is about the Houses of Lancaster, York, and Tudor (and Stuart) and their tribal feuds and dynastic wars.

(See Friedrich Nietzsche, *The Birth of Tragedy*, 1882; Francis Fergusson, *The Idea of a Theatre,* 1949; Susanne K. Langer, *Feeling and Form*, 1953; George Steiner, *The Death of Tragedy*, 1961; Eric Bentley, *The Life of the Drama*, 1964; Robert W. Corrigan, *Tragedy: Vision and Form*, 1965.)

TRAGIC FLAW

(See *hamartia*)

TRAGICOMEDY

(See **figure 1: "The Ur Drama, Winter"**) Throughout history playwrights have attempted to create a synthesis of the two visions of the human condition (see **comedy, tragedy**). Against this desire has been the purist (and elitist) notion that the two genres should reflect the strict division of social classes. Aristotle separated comedy and tragedy on the basis of class (disguised as levels of goodness)[102] and

---

[102]Aristotle, *Poetics*, chapter II, 1448a, 1-20.

neoclassic theorists, tied to absolutist patrons, decreed that the two forms should not be mixed.[103]

Elizabethan dramatists not only mixed classes in both tragedies and comedies, they also attempted to mix comic and tragic elements. The results were plays which might have potentially tragic characters, but which end happily (as in *Measure for Measure*), or potentially comic characters (as Lear and the Fool in *King Lear,* Mercutio in *Rome and Juliet*), but end tragically. The Jacobean playwrights were fond of writing tragedies with happy endings, and John Fletcher defined the form for his age by describing it as a tragedy without death, but not a comedy because several characters come close to it.[104] **Melodrama** adopts a similar strategy by threatening "hellfire and damnation," but contriving positive endings--thus reflecting middle class social tactics and positive expectations. (see **poetic justice**).

Modern tragicomedy, however, emerged with the triumph of a relativistic world view. It is essentially an ironic vision as Frye points out,[105] one which pictures characters as distinctly average and helpless individuals caught in a web of absurd social relationships. It is a vision with a dual perspective: the funny and the sad, the absurd and the frightening, the pathetic and the grotesque are mixed, not so much on the stage, but in the audience's perceptions of character behaviour.

Chekhov was the first modern master of the genre, although Ibsen had portrayed the essence of the tragicomic hero in *The Wild Duck*. In the *Cherry Orchard* Chekhov has a cast of characters who are totally lost in helpless, pathetic subjectivity, unable to see themselves in context. Only the audience, given the perspective of the big picture, can sympathize with individual pain, but simultaneously appreciate ludicrous behaviour.

---

[103]Note, however, that Giovanni Battista Guarini (1538-1612) argued in favour of a possible mixture of comedy and tragedy: see "Compendium of Tragicomic Poetry," in Dukore, *Dramatic Theory and Criticism*, pp. 150-155.

[104]John Fletcher, preface to *The Faithful Shepherdess*, 1610.

[105]Northrop Frye, *Anatomy of Criticism*, Third Essay: "Archetypal Criticism."

(See Karl S. Guthke, *Modern Tragicomedy*, 1966; David L. Hirst, *Tragicomedy*, 1984; John Orr, *Tragicomedy and Contemporary Culture*, 1991.)

TRICKSTER

(See **farce**) A cross cultural, recurrent figure who appears in legend, fiction and drama; an **archetypal** spirit of anarchy and fun; a life-affirming force whose function is to puncture pretension and disturb complacency; appearing in many disguises, the trickster is a **displacement** of the "shapeshifter" of shamanic legend, witchcraft lore and classical mythology.[106] Shapeshifting, however, is just one aspect of the Trickster's fundamental skill, **improvisation,** which is the survival skill *par excellence*. (See Carl Jung, *Four Archetypes: Mother, Rebirth, Spirit, Trickster*, 1959.)

TRILOGY

In the dramatic festivals of Athens during the fifth century and later, playwrights were required to present three tragedies in the competition, and these were usually followed by a **satyr play**. More generally, however, a trilogy is a *series* of three plays on a common theme or on the lives of common characters (e.g., Sophocles' Theban trilogy, Shakespeare's Henry plays or James Reaney's Donnelly trilogy).

As to why three should be a more appropriate number than two or four, it is a matter of speculation on the universal human penchant for the number three as applied to works of art. A play is a "whole" which has a beginning, middle and end,[107] the first major interval is a third, a triad is a chord of three notes, a symphony has three movements (and a coda), a triptych was a common form of altarpiece in the Renaissance, and so on. In some of these cases, each one of the three parts is able to

---

[106]Pennethorne Hughes, *Witchcraft* (London: Longmans, Green, 1952), Part One, pp.35-56

[107]Aristotle, *Poetics*, 1451a, chapter 7, 25-32.

stand on its own as a "complete" work.

TRIO

(See **duet, quartet**) By adding just one character to a two character play, the playwright increases the number of possible character configurations from four to eight:

```
0.....................................................(empty stage)
(A), (B), (C).....................................(as solos)
A+B, A+C, B+C..............................(as duets)
A+B+C.............................................(as a trio)
```

These additional relationships facilitate both **subtext** and **dramatic irony** by presenting a dual perspective on the third character in a scene or in the play as a whole.

The loss of the duet's intimacy is compensated by the trio's greater versatility. The third character has several possible dramaturgical functions: the third can be an onlooker, a judge, a referee, a manipulator, the object of competition between the other two, an outsider and/or a person who changes sides.

TRITAGONIST

(Greek: "third character in the contest") In the Greek theatre, a third character is not the same as a third actor: full masks facilitated the inclusion of several characters played by just two actors. However, until Sophocles "invented" the third *actor*, a **trio** was not possible on the Greek stage.

TROPE

Strictly in reference to theatre history, any interpolation of text or music (or both) into the liturgy (church service). Thus, anything from an embellished note under a word in a hymn or chant (e.g., "alleluia" stretched from four syllables to many) to a playlet such as the ***Quem Quaeritis*** is a trope. In **rhetoric**, a trope refers to figures of speech and other literary embellishments, such as metaphor and allegory.

TURNING POINT

That point in an **action** where a character's "fortune" changes with finality (see **climax**).

TYPE

(See *figura*) Also, type (or "stereotype") refers to simply drawn characters, especially in **comedy** and **melodrama**, which are barely displaced from their **archetypes**. The opposite of a character type is a naturalistic character: that is, a unique individual, shaped by specific environmental and hereditary forces.

U

UNITIES

The "three unities" of **time**, place and **action** are the consequence of **neoclassic** rationalism. Given the fundamental principle of **verisimilitude** (truth to "Nature"), it follows that an action taking more time than it takes to watch it strains belief; that an action taking place in more than one location while the audience remains seated is also unbelievable; and most importantly, that an action which lacks **unity** and/ or which attempts to accomplish more than a single goal offends reason.

In their commentaries on Aristotle, humanist writers such as Scaliger (1484-1558: *Poetics*, 1561) and Castelvetro (1505-1571: *On Aristotle's Poetics*, 1570) went much further than their ancient master by insisting on a poetics (**dramaturgy**) based on abstract universals which would govern arts. In other words, they took the giant step from descriptive writing--merely translating and commenting on Aristotle and others--to prescriptive criticism. In this particular instance, a play was judged according to its adherence to their prescriptive rules. The logical extension of this policy would have been a drama in which time and space are irrelevant. (See **figure 9: "Neoplatonism and the Great Chain of Being"**.)

UNITY

According to Aristotle, an **action** is "complete" if it has a beginning, a middle, and an end."[108] A beginning is that which requires nothing before it: the

---

[108]Aristotle, *Poetics*, chapter 7, 1451a, 24-33.

action of Sophocles' *Oedipus* begins near the end of the *story* and this requires some **exposition** to recount the events and decisions which led up to this point. However, the action *of the play itself* requires nothing before the initial incident, the arrival of the Supplicants. A middle is that which is causally connected to the incidents which come before and to those which follow. An end is that which requires nothing further to complete the action.

Unity in a work of art therefore implies something more than mere "completeness." It implies that the parts of the work relate to each other with coherence, with nothing missing and nothing further needed. In a sense, modern drama and art begin when this notion of unity is challenged. Examples of modern "disunity" might include a painting which seems incomplete by referring to something off the frame; when the parts of a work seem unrelated to others; when a piece of music does not return to the base key; or when, as in some of Ibsen's plays, the ending does not "complete" the action, but suspends it, leaving the audience with a portentious question (see the ending of *Hedda Gabler*).

UPSTAGE

(See **down stage**) The direction away from the audience. The term comes from the stages of the Renaissance/Baroque periods which were raked (sloped) rather steeply toward the back of the stage to accomodate perspective scenery. This meant that the actual playing space was limited to a relatively narrow strip across the front of the stage. To "upstage" a fellow actor, move upstage of him so that, in order to face you, he must turn his back on the audience (such a move is normally counterproductive and therefore to be avoided).

UR DRAMA

(See **figure 1: "The Ur Drama"**) A phrase which refers to a purely theoretical, even fanciful, original "play-of-the-world." Schematically, it is divided into four mythic archetypes based on the cyclical nature of life and their corresponding ritual enactments ("Ur Dramas").

The notion of the Ur Drama is used in two ways: the first is that it is simply an organizing paradigm of dramatic literature based on a survey of the field;[109] the second is that it is a plausible explanation not only of the content of drama, but also of the origins of both drama and theatre. This theory states, in general, that theatre is a ritual enactment of myth (making imaginative truth *present*), and that myth is a culture's explanation of man's relationships--human, natural and spiritual.

(See E.T. Kirby, *The Ur Drama: the Origins of Theatre*, 1975; David Cole, *The Theatrical Event*, 1975; Mircea Eliade, *The Myth of the Eternal Return*, 1954; Theodore H. Gaster, *Thespis: Ritual Myth and Drama in the Ancient Near East*, 1950.)

UT PICTURA POESIS

(Latin: "poetry is like a picture") Although not intended in this sense by Horace,[110] in the Renaissance (and since) the phrase has come to infer fundamental similarities among the arts. Pictures are like poems (and *vice versa*), "tone poems," dance as "sculpture in motion," painting is "frozen music" are all ideas referring to the same phenomenon. In essence, all of the arts are responses to the life experience by artists who merely use different modes of communication. The principles of artistic creation, therefore, are analogous. References to pace or volume in theatre are similar to tempo and dynamics in music; stage pictures are figurative "snap shots" of the action; *tableau vivants* are living stage pictures; stage composition is merely pictorial composition in three dimensions with similar concerns for line, mass, texture, focus, contrast and rhythm. Alternatively, staged drama, complete with setting, properties, costumes, lighting and music and dance could never be a unified expression if the various "arts" involved were incompatible.

---

[109]After Northrop Frye's "Archetypal Criticism," see *Anatomy of Criticism*, 1958.

[110]Horace. *Ars Poetica (The Art of Poetry)*, in Dukore, *Dramatic Theory and Criticism*, trans. by Edward Henry Blakeney, p. 74.

V

VAUDEVILLE

Originally a French form of popular farce punctuated with popular songs and dances (see the English **Ballad Opera**).

Similar to the English music hall entertainment, vaudeville evolved from rough, bawdy, bar room shows to "family" entertainment through the 19th century in America, when Tony Pastor opened his 14th street theatre in New York in 1881. For a relatively small price working class people could see a variety of events, from pop songs and dances to dog acts and jugglers, from comic skits and routines to short melodramas and even sermons. As family entertainment for middle class customers, vaudeville attempted to exclude chorus lines and bawdy humour and to include the trappings of luxury. When the nickelodeons began competing for the entertainment dollar, vaudeville included film clips and newsreels.

It was ultimately the genius of **musical comedy** which synthesized many of these elements with original music and drama. Even before the musical had reached its mature form, however, vaudeville was defeated by higher ticket prices and motion pictures. Many of the stars of both stage and screen (and early TV) received their training in the vaudeville school of hard knocks. (See **revue**.)

(See R.W. Snyder, *The Voice of the City: Vaudeville and Popular Culture in New York*, 1989; Robert C. Toll, *On With the Show: the First Century of Show Business in America*, 1976.)

VERFREMDUNGSEFFEKT

(German: "estrangement," "making strange," "alienation effect." See **epic**

theatre; see also **figure 6.**) A basic principle of epic theatre and **modernism** (in general), *verfremdungseffekt* simply refers to any technique by which an observer of art can be given a momentary or sudden objective or critical perspective. The intention behind the principle is to break the seductive power of illusionism and empathy which (to Brecht, at least) weaken critical thought. Events, characters, situations and critical moments in the action are suddenly "made strange" by the actors, who might momentarily step out of their roles; by lighting effects; by the appearance of film strips behind the action; or by titles travelling from one side of the stage to another on a clothesline.

VERISIMILITUDE

(See **neoclassicism** and **figure 9**) One of the clearest short summaries of the principles of verisimilitude can be found in Oscar Brockett's *History of the Theatre*, sixth edition, 1991. Basically, the term refers to the fundamental principle of neoclassic **rhetoric**, namely, that art should be true to "nature." Nature, in neoplatonic thought, was an abstract universal, not the particulars of sense experience. It was therefore the function of art to imitate (to make concrete) the universal *norms* of value, truth and human behaviour. Put another way, art should expose the universal truth behind everyday detail.

This concept is by no means limited to Renaissance and Baroque humanism and art. The romantics, for example, expounded their version of ideal art being superior to changing nature: "'beauty is truth, truth beauty,'--that is all Ye know on earth, and all ye need to know."[111] What is abstract art but an attempt to bypass the imitation of particulars and portray essences?

VICE

(See **trickster**) The medieval "vice figure," in various disguises, appeared

---

[111]John Keats, *Ode on a Grecian Urn*, 1819: V, 49-50.

in **mysteries** and **moralities**, usually as a wicked, but entertaining "devil's disciple." One of the most famous of these is Mak, in the Wakefield *Second Shepherd's Play*, who disguises himself as nobility in order to fool the simple shepherds (unsuccessfully) and then renews his pact with Satan while they sleep.

VILLAIN

The **vice** figure of melodrama; the personification of evil to a middle class audience; often a rich man with a smooth tongue, who voices the proper moral sentiments while plotting to seduce the heroine and steal her fortune.

Interestingly, the villain, with close ancestors in Edmund (*King Lear*), Iago (*Othello*) and several others, continued the tradition of self justification. As the one major character in the cast who had more than one dimension and who flirted with evil, the villain was bound to explain his actions in terms which might not convince, but which would at least maintain the mystery of his behaviour. Similarly, in a cast of enervating goodness, the villain or villainess (*femme fatale*) and their cretinous henchmen were often the main sources of entertainment.

W

WEIMAR CLASSICISM

A name given to the work and goals of Goethe and Schiller at the Weimar Court Theatre from roughly 1791-1817. Both had turned their backs on the proto **romanticism** of the *sturn und drang* movement in order to advance their versions of a modified **neoclassicism**. Goeth'e *Iphegenia in Tauris* (1787) and Schiller's *Maria Stuart* (1800) illustrate their different, but complementary approaches to this objective. Goethe used the Greek myth as a framework for a discussion of fundamental problems in human relationships; Schiller focused on the major confrontations of history ("existential moments"), such as that between Mary Stuart and Elizabeth Tudor, Joan of Arc and the Catholic church, the legendary Wilhelm Tell and Dictatorship. In spite of their programme, however, the works of these writers, especially *Mary Stuart* and Goethe's *Faust*, betray their romantic idealism and fascination with the tragedy of "greatness" and heroic rebellion.

WELL-MADE PLAY

(From the French: *"piece bien faite"*) A dramaturgical formula for commercial success developed by the prolific French playwright, Eugene Scribe (1791-1861). Essentially a simplification of solid playwrighting techniques in practice since the Greeks combined with commercial common sense, the principles of the well-made play included:

1. Clear **exposition** at the beginning, usually conducted by servants

or a servant and a newcomer to the household.

2. An equally clear causal arrangement of incidents, with much use of coincidence which, while logically possible, was not predictable.

3. An action of rising tension within each scene, Act and play as a whole, which produced rises and falls in tension and the buildup of suspence.

4. Simplified characterization based on well recognized models in contemporary society; clear moral values (from **melodrama**); much intrigue and a clever use of incriminating letters or other props.

The formula of the well-made play became a formula of commercial success and was consequently widely influential. It was developed at a time when the popular commerical arts, through new technology and a brioadly based paying public, took a distinctly different path than the arts of either the establishment or the *avant garde*. The formula was perfected by Ibsen and Shaw and a few others who eliminated the no longer acceptable dramaturgy of **asides** and **soliloquys**, minimized coincidences which stretched credulity, deepened characterization and based their plots on profound social problems. The formula lives on today in television dramas and sitcoms.

(See Marvin Carlson, *The French Stage in the 19th Century*, 1972; Neil E. Arvin, *Eugene Scribe and the French Theatre, 1815-60*, 1924; George Bernard Shaw, *The Quintessence of Ibsenism*, 1895.)

WORKERS' THEATRE

This includes any theatre or drama by, for and/or about workers in the modern world ("workers" in the sense of "proletariat;" that is, since Marx); it also designates a specific movement in the '20s and '30s in the United States branching out from the work of the Workers' Drama League in 1926 (which later became the professional Theatre Union). By extension the term includes similar movements in other countries (such as Brecht and Piscator's Workers' Theatre in Germany) in response to similar concerns of workers during the heydays of "boss capitalism" and the Great

Depression. All of these movements and organizations and the work they produced were strongly "counter-ideological," that is, they attempted to replace decades of capitalistic conditioning with a different political and economic world view. As marginal theatre movements, most were opposed by the establishment, most tended to be preachy and boring and most were short lived. A few, however, produced profound theatrical experiences which have not lost their interest or value; later plays of "social significance" by major playwrights were strongly influenced by the movement; and in general north American theatre "came of age" politically as a result of Workers' Theatre. (See **alternative theatre.**)

More specifically, the Federal Theatre Project in the United States was initiated partially in response to the demands of the Workers' Theatre movement; the Theatre Guild and the Group Theatre and the "golden age" of American theatre in the '30s and '40s were all influenced by the social consciousness of workers' theatre. Successful examples of American workers' theatre include: Clifford Odets' *Waiting for Lefty,* 1935; the musical revue, *Pins and Needles,* 1933, by the Ladies Garment Workers' Union; Marc Blitzstein's outlawed *The Cradle Will Rock,* 1937.

(See Eugene van Erven, *Radical People's Theatre,* 1988; I. Levine, *Left Wing Dramatic Theory in the American Theatre,* 1986; Samuel Raphael, ed., *Theatres of the Left, 1880-1935,* 1985; Morgen Y. Himelstein, *When Drama was a Weapon: Left-Wing Theatre in New York, 1929-41,* 1976; Malcolm Goldstein, *The Political Stage: American Theatre and Drama of the Great Depression,* 1971; Harold Clurman, *The Fervent Years: The Story of the Group Theatre and the Thirties,* 1983.)

A very useful summary of the Canadian Workers' Theatre movement, along with numerous bibliographical references, can be found in the Introduction to *Eight Men Speak, and Other Plays from the Canadian Workers' Theatre,* 1976, by Robin Endres; see also, Toby G. Ryan, *Stage Left: Canadian Theatre in the Thirties,* 1981.

Z

ZANNI

(See **commedia dell'arte**) Strictly, the two male comic servants, one wiley (Brighella), the other an incompetent clown (Arrlechino); broadly, a class of comic servants.

ZARZUELA

A Spanish form of musical comedy with ancient roots in folk drama and in the theatrical entertainments commissioned by Philip IV in his palace of the same name. The Zarzuela has spoken dialogue, some original music and some popular songs. It is still popular today.

ZAUBERSTUCK

(German: "flute play") A form which mixes fantasy and realism with music, either in farce or in opera (as in Mozart's *Die Zauberflote*, "The Magic Flute").

THE "UR DRAMA"[1]

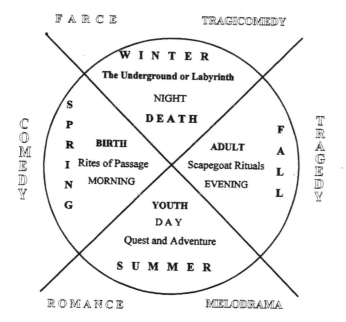

Figure 1

[1]This diagram is a visual interpretation (and adaptation for drama) of the paradigm suggested by Northrop Frye, *Anatomy of Criticism*, 1957.

A LIST OF DRAMATIC AND THEATRICAL RELATIONSHIPS

The dramaturgical significance of this list will be appreciated if questions like the following are asked: "what is the relationship between this *Text* and the *Idea* behind it, or between this *Text* (as a whole) and this (specific) *Issue*, or between this line of *Text* and its *Subtext*?"

Text / Idea
Text / Issue
Text / Subtext
Text / performance text
Text / Mise en scene
Text / Society (synchrony)
Text / History (diachrony)

Actor / Text
Actor / Style
Actor / Subtext (role)
Actor / Actor
Actor / Stage
Actor / Offstage
Actor / Properties
Actor / Costume
Actor / Audience

Character / Objective
Character / Issues
Character / Situation
Character / Character
Character / Environment (on stage)
Character / Environment (offstage)
Character / Objects
Character / Clothing
Character / Time
Character / Audience

Onstage / Offstage
Stage / Auditorium
Auditorium / Theatre
Theatre / City

Figure 2

THE DRAMATURGY OF THEATRE RELATIONSHIPS

The following four diagrams focus attention on the interface between some of the dramaturgical pairs listed in **figure 2**. The Text / Idea relationship is seen as central to all other pairs, with the **style** of one pair affecting the style others and thus creating theatrical styles, such as **realism, expressionism** and **epic theatre**.

ACTORS / AUDIENCE	CHARACTER / AUDIENCE
ACTORS / STAGE	CHARACTER / ENVIRONMENT
ACTOR / ROLE	CHARACTER / BEHAVIOUR
ACTOR / ACTOR	CHARACTER / CHARACTER
PERFORMANCE / SOCIETY	CHARACTER / SOCIETY

Figure 3

THE DRAMATURGY OF THEATRE RELATIONSHIPS

REALISM

The **TEXT** is proposed as an objective record, carefully researched; the **IDEA** springs from sense experience and observation.

Actors do not relate to audience

| ACTORS / AUDIENCE |

Characters do not relate to audience

| CHARACTER / AUDIENCE |

Actors create an illusion

| ACTORS / STAGE |

Character seen in natural context

| CHARACTER / ENVIRONMENT |

Research: close identification

| ACTOR / ROLE |

Shaped by environment & heredity

| CHARACTER / BEHAVIOUR |

Treat each other as characters

| ACTOR / ACTOR |

Socially defined relationships (class)

| CHARACTER / CHARACTER |

Tends toward the documentary

| PERFORMANCE / SOCIETY |

The individual is part of a system of laws

| CHARACTER / SOCIETY |

Figure 4

THE DRAMATURGY OF THEATRE RELATIONSHIPS

EXPRESSIONISM

The **TEXT** is a scream of protest / anguish; the **IDEA** springs from personal anguish and feelings of alienation and /or persecution.

Actors confront audience

ACTORS / AUDIENCE

No relationship (unless presentational)

CHARACTER / AUDIENCE

The stage as an expressive machine

ACTORS / STAGE

Places are projections of inner states

CHARACTER / ENVIRONMENT

Artist's personal expression

ACTOR / ROLE

Subconscious drives are foremost

CHARACTER / BEHAVIOUR

A team of performers

ACTOR / ACTOR

Elemental conflicts (e.g., male / female)

CHARACTER / CHARACTER

Performance as rebellion/social protest

PERFORMANCE / SOCIETY

Alienated individuals in hostile society

CHARACTER / SOCIETY

Figure 5

THE DRAMATURGY OF THEATRE RELATIONSHIPS

BRECHTIAN or "EPIC"

The **TEXT** as "gestic language" and illustrative parable; the **IDEA** is a basic ideological premise with a social objective.

Actors as teachers of contemporaries

> **ACTORS / AUDIENCE**

As a *character*, no relationship

> **CHARACTER / AUDIENCE**

Working space / lecture platform

> **ACTORS / STAGE**

Conditioning forces are specific to time & place

> **CHARACTER / ENVIRONMENT**

Objective demonstrator

> **ACTOR / ROLE**

Historical / ideological conditioning

> **CHARACTER / BEHAVIOUR**

Ideological colleagues

> **ACTOR / ACTOR**

Historically conditioned relationships (class)

> **CHARACTER / CHARACTER**

Dialectical propositions to effect change

> **PERFORMANCE / SOCIETY**

Characters have no social objectivity

> **CHARACTER / SOCIETY**

Figure 6

DRAMATURGICAL DATA
(Summary)
Henrik Ibsen's *HEDDA GABLER*[2]

These tables facilitate comparisons between character speech (lines per act) and **presence** (pages per Act), **french scenes** and character combinations (duets, trios, quartets per act).

SPEECH	I	II	III	IV	TOTAL
HEDDA	174	275	163	136	748
TESMAN	231	92	73	138	534
BRACK	50	145	80	94	369
THEA	140	36	60	49	285
LOEVBORG	—	135	65	—	200
AUNT JULIA	140	—	—	40	18

Total Lines (approx.):　2350

PRESENCE	I	II	III	IV	TOTAL
HEDDA	28	27	16	17	80
TESMAN	22	17	5	13	57
BRACK	5	26	5	12	48
THEA	10	7	6	9	32
LOEVBORG	—	15	7	—	22
AUNT JULIA	12	—	—	3	15

Fr. scenes / page:　17/29　14/27　16/18　14/17　61/91

Duets:	6	3	7	3	19
Trios:	5	2	4	2	13
Quartets:	1	1	----	1	3

Figure 7

---

[2]Henrik Ibsen *Hedda Gabler*, trans. by Michael Meyer (New York: Methuen, 1956).

240

FRENCH SCENES: GRAPHIC DISPLAY

Henrik-Ibsen's Hedda Gabler

The play's text as a whole: 62 scenes in 98 pp.

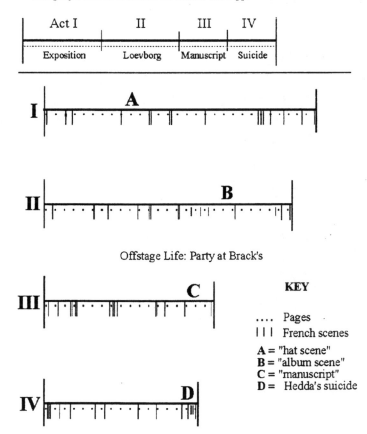

Offstage Life: Party at Brack's

Figure 8 (A)

HEDDA GABLER
Graphic Display: French Scene Composition

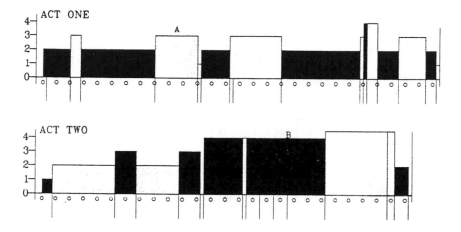

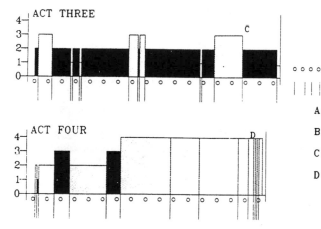

KEY

o o o o   Pages

| | | | French Scenes

A   "hat scene"

B   "album scene"

C   "manuscript"

D   Hedda's suicide

Figure 8A

NEOPLATONISM AND THE GREAT CHAIN OF BEING[3]

GOD-IN-HEAVEN	DIVINE JUSTICE	DIVINE BEAUTY
CHRIST	DIVINE GOODNESS	UNIVERSALS
ARCHANGELS	EVERLASTING PEACE	PURE FORMS
ANGELS	ANGELIC COURTS	ORDER & HARMONY
SAINTS	SPRITUAL LOVE	CELESTIAL BEAUTY

MAN-ON-EARTH	HUMAN JUSTICE	EARTHLY BEAUTY
KINGS POPES NOBLES CARDINALS GENTLEMEN BISHOPS MERCHANTS CLERGY PEASANTS FLOCK SLAVES HEATHENS	VIRTUE (Honour, Duty, Courage)	ARTS music poetry painting sculpture architecture
	DECORUM (Behaviour)	
ANIMALS pets beasts insects	PLATONIC LOVE (friendship, loyalty) PROFANE LOVE	RHETORIC *inventio* *dispositio* *ethopoea* *expressio*
PLANTS domestic weeds	APPETITE SIN	CRAFTS
MINERALS gold silver gems stones	INJUSTICE EVIL	UGLINESS dissonance imbalance CHAOS

Figure 9

[3]This diagram, as such, is original. It owes much, however, to Arthur O. Lovejoy, *The Great Chain of Being: a Study in the History of an Idea* (Cambridge: Harvard Univ. Press, 1966) and to Paul Oskar Kristeller, *The Philosophy of Marcilio Ficino* (New York: Scribner's, 1943).

SINGLE POINT PERSPECTIVE AND RENAISSANCE THEATRE

Parallel lines *appear* to converge in the distance: from a central vanishing point (**VP**) on the **horizon line**. Transferring a three dimensional scene to a two dimensional

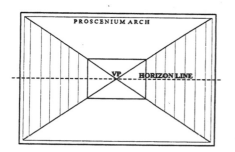

medium (paper, canvas) creates an *illusion* of reality. Objects recede toward the vanishing point on a proportionate grid. Objects thus appear relatively larger or smaller according to their distance from the picture plane.

Note that the vanishing point can be moved up or down or from side to side by the designer, who in this way controls the ideal spot to view the painting or stage.

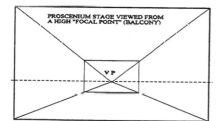

A proscenium arch stage was thus seen as a giant picture frame within which scenery could be designed according to the principles of "scientific" perspective. The major problem was the human actor's inability to "shrink" at the same rate as the scenery as he moved from the picture plane toward the vanishing point. He became confined to a relatively narrow strip of stage *in front of* the scenery.

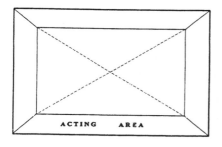

Renaissance painting, however, became interested in the possibilities of penetrating the distance beyond the picture plane toward *multiple* vanishing points. At this time, painting and stage design parted company. Courtly **decorum** required that only one focal point should exist in the auditorium. The exception to this rule is the *Teatro Olympico* (Vincenza, 1584) with its three perspective streets. This theatre, however, was built in a humanist academy. The models for court theatre designers were Serlio's three perspective scenes (tragedy, comedy and pastoral). (See Oscar Brockett, *History of the Theatre*, 6th ed., 1991.)

Figure 10

PRINCIPLES OF THE NEOCLASSIC STAGE

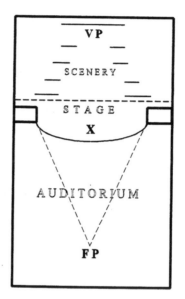

Theoretically, the scenery is a projection of an *ideal reality*, from a focal point (**FP**) in the seat of honour (the "Godly Prince"). The hero of this ideal space (**X**), standing directly downstage of the vanishing point (**VP**), is thus visually equated with the Godly Prince at the focal point: the hero is to his space as the Prince is to the court and the state. Just as the hero/actor is a virtuoso performer on stage, so the Prince is a virtuoso ruler in the world.

The stage, according to these principles, is an idealized extension of the courtly world. The scenery and the auditorium are designed so that seats other than the Prince's are by degrees inferior in social as well as aesthetic terms. This theatre is a thoroughly class structured space.

Figure 11

THE HISTORY OF FESTIVE THEATRE

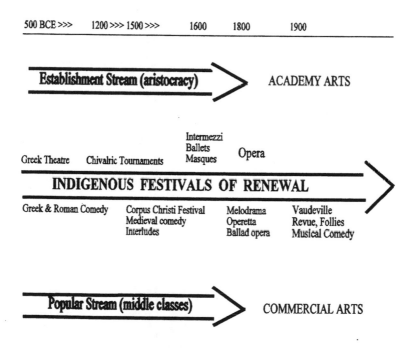

Figure 12

PERIODICITY

The illustrated periods are valid for European culture only; time spans are approximate and overlap, depending on location ((i.e., whether northern or southern Europe).

600 BCE to 400 AD	to	800	to	1000	to	1400	to	1600	to	1800	to	1900	to	2000

CLASSICAL   **MEDIEVAL**   **RENAISSANCE**   **MODERN**

archaic / classical   early Christian / Carolingian / Romanesque / gothic   romantic   modern   postmodern
Hellenic / Roman   early / high / mannerist / baroque

Figure 13

SELECTED BIBLIOGRAPHY

General References

Allen, Ralph G. and John Gassner. *Theatre and Drama in the Making.* 2 vols. Boston: Houghton Mifflin, 1964.

Apel, Willi. *Harvard Dictionary of Music. 2nd ed.* Cambridge: Harvard Univ. Press, 1979.

Banham, Martin, ed. *The Cambridge Guide to the Theatre.* rev. ed. New York: Cambridge Univ. Press, 1992.

Benson, Eugene and L.W. Conolly, eds. *The Oxford Companion to Canadian Theatre, The.* Toronto: Oxford Univ. Press, 1989.

Bordman, Gerald. *American Musical Theatre, a Chronicle.* Expanded Ed. New York: Oxford Univ. Press, 1986.

Brockett, Oscar. *History of the Theatre.* 6th ed. New York: Allyn and Bacon, 1991.

Carlson, Marvin. *Theories of the Theatre: a Historical and Critical Survey, from the Greeks to the Present.* Ithaca: Cornell Univ. Press, 1984.

Clark, Barrett H., ed.: *European Theories of the Theatre. European Theories of the Drama.* Revised by Henry Popkin. New York: Crown, 1965.

Clarke, Mary and David Vaughan, eds. *The Encyclopedia of Dance and Ballet.* London: Peerage Books, 1977.

Dukore, Bernard F. *Dramatic Theory and Criticism: Greeks to Grotowski.* New York: Holt, Rinehart and Winston, 1974.

Frye, Northrop, Sheridan Baker and George Perkins. *The Harper Handbook to Literature.* New York: Harper and Row, 1985.

Gowans, Allen. *Learning to See: Historical Perspectives on Modern Popular Commercial Arts.* Bowling Green: Bowling Green Univ. Popular Press, 1981.

Grout, Donald J. *A History of Western Music.* Rev. ed. New York: W.W. Norton, 1960.

Hartnol, *Phyllis. The Oxford Companion to the Theatre*. 3rd. ed. London: Oxford Univ. Press, 1972.

Hauser, Arnold. *The Social History of Art.* Stanley Godman, trans. 4 vols. London: Routledge and Kegan Paul, 1962 (1951).

Hindley, Geoffrey, ed. *Larousse Enclyclopedia of Music.* London: Hamlyn, 1971.

Jones, David E. and Jack Halstead. *A Dictionary of Dramaturgical Terms.* Unpublished.

Murray, Peter and Linda. *A Dictionary of Art and Artists.* Harmondsworth, Middlesex: Penguin, 1960.

Nagler, A.M. *A Source Book in Theatrical History.* New York: Dover, 1952.

Norwich, John Julius, ed. *Oxford Illustrated Encyclopedia of the Arts.* New York: Oxford Univ. Press, 1990.

Mondadori, Arnoldo, ed. *Simon & Schuster Book of the Opera.* New York: Simon and Schuster, 1978.

Taylor, John Russell. *Penguin Dictionary of the Theatre.* Harmondsworth, Middlesex: Penguin, 1966.

Wilmeth, Don B. and Tice L. Miller. *Cambridge Guide to American Theatre.* New York: Cambridge Univ. Press, 1993.

Histories

Arnott, Peter D. *Public and Performance in the Greek Theatre*. London: Routledge, 1989.

_____*Greek Scenic Conventions*. Westport, Conn.: Greenwood Press, 1979 (1962).

Benson, Eugene and L.W. Conolly. *English Canadian Theatre*. Toronto: Oxford Univ. Press, 1987.

Bieber, Margarete. *The History of the Greek and Roman Theatre*, 2nd ed. Princeton, N.J.: Prtinceton Univ. Press, 1961.

Bigsby, C.W.E. *A Critical Introduction to Twentieth Century American Drama*. 3 vols. Cambridge: Cambridge Univ. Press, 1985.

Booth, Micheal R. *Theatre in the Victorian Age*. New York: Cambridge Univ. Press, 1991.

Brockett, Oscar G. and Robert R. Findlay. *Century of Innovation: a History of European and American Theatre and Drama Since 1870*. Englewood Cliffs, N.J.: Prentice-Hall, 1973.

Brown, Frederick. *Theatre and Revolution*. New York: Viking, 1980.

Chambers, E.K. *The Medieval Stage*. 2 vols. London: Oxford Univ. Press, 1903.

Donington, Robert. *The Opera*. New York: Harcourt Brace Jovanovich, 1978.

Erven, Eugene van. *Radical People's Theatre*. Bloomington: Indiana Univ. Press, 1988.

Filewod, Allen. *Collective Encounters: Documentary Theatre in English Canada*. Toronto: Univ. of Toronto Press, 1987.

Gardner, John. *The Construction of the Wakefield Cycle*. Carbondale: Southern Illinois Univ. Press, 1974.

Grout, Donald J. *A Short History of the Opera*. 2nd ed. New York: 1965 (1947).

Martines, Lauro. *Power and Imagination: City States in Renaissance Italy*. New York: Knopf, 1978.

250

McNair, Peter L. "Kwakiutl Winter Dances," in *Arts Canada: Stones, Bones and Skin, Ritual and Shamanic Art*, Volume XXX, nos. 5 and 6

Nagler, A.M. *Theatre Festivals of the Medici*. New Haven: Yale Univ. Press, 1964.

Nelson, Alan H. *The Medieval English Stage: Corpus Christi Pageants and Plays*. Chicago: Univ. of Chicago Press, 1974.

Samuel, Raphael, Ewan MacColl and Stuart Cosgrove. *Theatres of the Left, 1880-1935: Workers' Theatre Movements in Britain and America*. History Workshop Series. London: Routledge and Kegan Paul, 1985.

Senelick, Laurence, ed. *National Theatre in Northern and Eastern Europe, 1746-1900*. Theatre in Europe: a Documentary History. New York: Cambridge Univ. Press, 1991.

Thomas, David, ed. *Restoration and Georgian England, 1660-1788*. Theatre in Europe: a Documentary History. New York: Cambridge Univ. Press, 1989.

Tydeman, William. *The Theatre in the Middle Ages: Western European Stage Conditions ca. 800-1575*. London: Cambridge Univ. Press, 1978.

Usmiani, Renate. *Second Stage: The Alternative Theatre Movement in Canada*. Vancouver: Univ. of B.C. Press, 1983.

Walton, Michael J. *Greek Theatre Practice*. Rev. ed. London: Methuen, 1991.

Wickham, Glynne. *The Medieval Theatre*. New York: St. Martin's Press, 1974.

_____. *Early English Stages: 1300 to 1660*. 2 vols. London: Routledge and Kegan Paul, 1963.

Yates, Frances A. *Astraea: the Imperial Theme in the Sixteenth Century*. London: Routledge and Kegan Paul, 1975.

Dramatic Theory, Dramaturgy

Abrams, M.H. *The Mirror and the Lamp: Romantic Theory and the Critical Tradition.* New York: W.W. Norton, 1953.

Anonymous. *Tractatus Coislinianus.* Trans. by Lane Cooper. In Dukore, *Dramatic Theory and Criticism: Greeks to Grotowski.* New York: Holt, Rinehart and Winston, 1974.

Aristotle. *Poetics.* Trans. by Ingram Bywater. New York: Random House, 1947.

Artaud, Artaud. *The Theatre and its Double.* New York: Grove Press, 1958.

Austin, G. *Feminist Theories for Drama Criticism.* Ann Arbor: Univ. of Michigan Press, 1990.

Barthes, Roland. *Critical Essays.* Trans. by Richard Howard. Evanston: University of Illinois, 1972.

Boal, *Augusto. Theatre of the Oppressed.* New York: Theatre Comm. Group, 1985.

Bradley, David. *From Text to Performance in the Elizabethan Theatre: Preparing the Play for the Stage.* New York: Cambridge Univ. Press, 1992.

Brater, Enoch and Ruby Cohn, eds. *Around the Absurd: Essays on Modern and Post Modern Drama.* Ann Arbor: University of Michigan Press, 1990.

Brecht, Bertolt. "A Little Organon for the Theatre." John Willet, trans. In John Willet, *Brecht on Theatre.* London: Methuen, 1964.

Burke, Kenneth. *A Rhetoric of Motives*, 2nd ed. New York: Scribners, 1969.

Carlson, Susan. *Women and Comedy: Re-writing the British Theatrical Tradition.* Ann Arbor: Univ. of Michigan Press, 1991.

Case, Sue Ellen. *Feminism and Theatre.* New York: Oxford Univ. Press, 1988.

Cohen, Robert. *Acting Power.* Irvine, Cal.: Mayfield, 1979.

Coleridge, Samuel Taylor. "Progress of the Drama." In Dukore, *Dramatic Theory and Criticism: Greeks to Grotowski.* New York: Holt, Rinehart and Winston, 1974.

_____. "Biographia Literaria," III, 6. In Dukore, *Dramatic Theory and Criticism: Greeks to Grotowski*. New York: Holt, Rinehart and Winston, 1974.

Collier, Jeremy. "A Short View of the Immorality and Profaneness of the English Stage. In Dukore, *Dramatic Theory and Criticism: Greeks to Grotowski*. New York: Holt, Rinehart and Winston, 1974.

Dryden, John. "Preface to an Evening's Love." In Dukore, *Dramatic Theory and Criticism: Greeks to Grotowski*. New York: Holt, Rinehart and Winston, 1974.

Elam, Kier. *The Semiotics of Theatre and Drama*. London: Methuen, 1980.

Esslin, Martin. *Theatre of the Absurd*. New York: Grove, 1960.

Fergusson, Francis. *The Idea of a Theatre*. New York: Doubleday, 1949.

Freytag, Gustave. *Techniques of Drama: an Exposition of Dramatic Composition and Art,* trans. by E.J. MacEwen. New York: Scribners, 1968.

Frye, Northrop. *Anatomy of Criticism: Four Essays*. Princeton: Princeton Univ. Press, 1957.

_____. *The Secular Scripture: a Study of the Structure of Romance*. Cambridge: Harvard Univ. Press, 1976.

Goldman, Michael. *The Actor's Freedom*: *Towards a New Theory of Drama*. New York: Anchor, 1975.

Grotowski, Jerzy. *Towards a Poor Theatre*. New York: Simon and Schuster, 1968.

Hardison, O.B. *Christian Rite and Christian Drama in the Middle Ages*. Baltimore: Johns Hopkins, 1965.

Horace. "The Art of Poetry." Trans. by Edward Henry Blakeney. In Bernard Dukore, ed., *Dramatic Theory and Criticism: Greeks to Grotowski*. New York: Holt, Rinehart and Winston, 1974.

Kirby, Michael. *Happenings: an Illustrated Anthology*. New York: Methuen, 1966.

Langer, Susan K. *Feeling and Form*. New York: Scribners, 1953.

Lillo, George. *The London Merchant*: *Dedication*. In Dougald MacMillan and Howard M. Jones, eds. *Plays of the Restoration and Eighteenth Century*. New

York: Holt, Rinehardt and Winston, 1931.

Marranca, Bonnie. *Theatre of Images*. New York: Performing Arts Books, 1977.

McConachie, Bruce A. "Towards a Postpositivist Theatre History," in *Theatre Journal*, December, 1985.

Murphy, Roland, S.J. "The Mass: a Ceremonial Ritual," in *The Spectrum of Ritual: a Biogenetic Structural Analysis*, Eugene G. d'Aquili, ed. New York: Columbia Univ. Press, 1979.

Pfister, Manfred. *The Theory and Analysis of Drama*, trans. by John Halliday. New York: Cambridge Univ. Press, 1988, (1977).

Schmit, Thomas. "A Fluxus Farewell to Perfection." An interview by Gunter Berghaus in *The Drama Review*, T141, Spring, 1944.

Stanislavsky, Constantin. *An Actor Prepares*, trans. by Elizabeth Reynolds Hapgood. New York: Theatre Arts Books, 1936.

Steele, Sir Richard. Prologue to "The Conscious Lovers." In *Plays of the Restoration and Eighteenth Century*. London: Oxford Univ. Press, 1954.

Wagner, Richard. "The Purpose of the Opera." In *European Theories of the Drama*, Barrett H. Clark, ed., revised by Henry Popkin. New York: Crown, 1965.

Zeami, Motokiyo. *Kadensho*. Trans. by Chuichi Sakurai. Kyoto: Sumiya-Shinobe, 1968.

254

Miscellaneous

Anglo, Sidney. *Spectacle, Pageantry and Early Tudor Policy*. London: Thames and Hudson, 1969.

Beckett, Samuel. *Proust.* New York: Grove, 1957.

Brandon, S.G.F. *Man and God in Art and Ritual: a Study of Iconography, Architecture and Ritual Action as Primary Evidence of Religious Belief & Practice*. New York: Scribner's, 1975.

Burris-Meyer, Harold and Edward C. Cole. *Theatres and Auditoriums*. New York: Krieger Publishing, 1975.

Dix, Dom Gregory. *The Shape of the Liturgy*. London: Daire Press, 1946.

Eliade, Mircea. *Shamanism: Archaic Techniques of Ecstasy*, trans. by Willard R. Trask. New Jersey: Princeton Univ. Press, 1964.

Froissart. *Chronicles* (ca. 1400), trans. by Geoffrey Brereton. Harmondsworth, Middlesex: Penguin, 1968.

Gennep, Arnold van. *The Rites of Passage*. Trans. by Monika B. Vizedom and Gabrielle L. Caffee. Chicago: Chicago Univ. Press, 1969.

Goffman, Erving. *Presentation of Self in Everyday Life*. New York: Doubleday, 1959.

Hodge, Francis. *Play Directing*, 3rd ed. Englewood Cliffs: Prentice Hall, 1988.

Hughes, Pennethorne. *Witchcraft*. London: Longmans, Green, 1952.

Levi-Strauss, Claude. *Structural Anthropology.* Trans. by Claire Jacobson and Brooke Grundfest Schoepf. New York: Basic Books, 1963.

Nolan, Barbara. *The Gothic Visionary Perspective.* Princeton: Princeton Univ. Press, 1977.

Panofsky, Erwin. *Early Netherlandish Painting, its Origins and Character*, vol. 1. New York: Harper and Row, 1971 (1953).

Wolfflin, Heinrich. *Classic Art*, 2nd ed. (London: Phaidon, 1953).